W.W. II ARMY NURSE

# June Houghton Sullivan

## A LIFE STORY

❧

GUNILLA CAULFIELD

ISBN-10: 1481896059
ISBN-13: 9781481896054

Library of Congress Control Number: 2013900350
CreateSpace Independent Publishing Platform
North Charleston, South Carolina

Also by Gunilla Caulfield:

FICTION:

*Reunification Express*
*The Wave*
*A Novel in the Time of Global Warming*
*The Bookseller and Other Stories*

THE ANNIE QUITNOT MYSTERIES:

*Murder on Bearskin Neck*
*Murder at Hammond Castle*
*Murder in Pigeon Cove*

DEDICATION:

To June, and to her children, grandchildren
and great-grandchildren.

To the soldiers, and to all those who care for the wounded
in a war zone.

And lastly, with all my love to my husband, Thomas,
who worked patiently on restoring the photos in this book.

AUTHOR'S NOTE:

This book is based on my personal interviews with June (Houghton) Sullivan in Rockport, Massachusetts, over the past two years. The images in the book are mainly from June's W.W.II photo album, along with a few family photos.

*Gunilla Caulfield*

# CONTENTS:

# CHAPTER ONE

# THE GRAY GHOST

January 24, 1943: President Roosevelt and Prime Minister Churchill meet in Casablanca.

February 11, 1943: General Eisenhower is selected to command Allied armies in Europe.

April 7, 1943: Gen. George S. Patton's forces join British Eighth Army in attack on the Afrika Korps.

April 19, 1943: Reports tell of Nazi annihilation of two million European Jews by gas chamber, mass execution.

*The Gray Ghost, New York Harbor*

To June's relief, all she saw in the sky was stars. Even in normal times, before part of the world lived in that depressing blackout darkness, the stars always seemed to sparkle more brightly out on the ocean. The absence of sweeping searchlights and ominous drone of approaching planes overhead was also comforting; the only sounds heard up on deck were the hum of the engines of the mammoth ship, and the pulsing of the waves briskly striking its hull. June Houghton, newly enlisted Army Corps nurse, shuddered in the night chill. Her hands gripped the railing, which was wet and cold. A slender, young woman just turned twenty-three, June still looked more like a girl, especially in this daunting setting. Her light-brown hair fluttered in the wind, slapping her cheeks.

People would call her pretty until she smiled and turned her eyes on them—eyes of a startlingly clear aquamarine with flecks of sea-green, ringed with an edge of silver—when suddenly she became beautiful. Now, in this dark, vast loneliness, she hugged herself, grasping her arms tightly. The thin-sleeved jacket wasn't enough to keep her warm, but the big winter coat would have taken up all the space in the small suitcase allowed. June suddenly missed her brother, Warren, until now the anchor in her life. Then, stubbornly, she pulled herself together and drew a last long breath of cool sea air before returning to her bunk area below deck.

When the *Gray Ghost* left New York Harbor on this crossing, in early June of 1943, the ship had been escorted for the first day by a number of vessels, but now, far out at sea, she was on her own. June and the other nurses had been assured that the ship was so fast that they need have no fear of German ships catching them. The passengers on the *Ghost* were not likely to be in any danger, except possibly from submarines. Hitler had offered a bounty of $250,000 and an Iron Cross to any U-boat captain who would sink her. There was a submarine watch—the ship had recently been fitted with an underwater sound-detection system, along with a mine-sweeping *paravane* system and a *degaussing girdle*, which was wrapped around the ship. The girdle was meant to neutralize magnetic mines. June hoped fervently that they wouldn't encounter any of those hazards and that they would have a safe crossing. She noticed that as the *Gray Ghost* made her way across the Atlantic, the ship began to zigzag. It would continue this defensive maneuver all the way across the Atlantic.

*The Gray Ghost at sea, loaded with troops.*

The *Gray Ghost* was really a war-time alias for the RMS *Queen Mary*. In 1939–1940, at the outbreak of the Second World War, the British Government Ministry of Shipping had called the magnificent ship up for duty. The bold Cunard Line red, black, and white exterior had been painted camouflage gray, and the ship had been renamed. The *Gray Ghost* was the largest troopship to sail in the war and could carry up to 17,000 troops at a speed of thirty knots. On this troopship crossing, the 1077th Signal Army Company Service Group, thousands of enlisted men, and a whole hospital of doctors, nurses, and corpsmen were on board. June and her unit, part of the 120th Station Hospital, soon found that the medical personnel on board had surged from all parts of the United States. June's newly made friends on the ship included Hazel Hearn, Nellie Vincomi, Frances Snitzler (they called her Snitty), Bette Benaud, Mary Ellen Edmonds, Grace Russell, Frances Melle and many others. Nellie and Snitty were both from Pennsylvania; Grace came from Maine, and Frances from Connecticut. June had bunked with Hazel since they first arrived at Camp Edwards in Massachusetts, where they had been assigned to their bunks alphabetically. Hazel was born in Connecticut and brought up in England before moving back to the States, and the two had made fast friends after recognizing their similar, nomadic pasts. Friendships lasting lifelong were born on board the *Gray Ghost*.

During the early part of the war, it had taken stubborn, hard work by a number of influential people to get the Women's Army Auxiliary Corps started, notably Congresswoman Edith Nourse Rogers, Eleanor Roosevelt, and General George

C. Marshall. It took General Marshall to finally order the War Department to create a women's corps.

When June signed up, in May of 1943, she was twenty-two years old, which was the minimum age at that time. The ANC's superintendent, Col. Julia O. Flikke, accepted only unmarried women, aged twenty-two to thirty, who had received their RN training from civilian schools. If a nurse married or became pregnant, she would be discharged.

The *Gray Ghost* would also serve as a means of transporting prisoners, wounded soldiers, and "very important passengers." On the way over to the States earlier in the year—from Gourock, Scotland, to New York—British Prime Minister Winston Churchill had been on board, headed for meetings with President Roosevelt and Allied Forces officials. On that, as on his other voyages on the *Gray Ghost,* Churchill was listed as "Colonel Walden." On those crossings, the Prime Minister and a large number of government officials enjoyed the use of staterooms in the sumptuous style of the RMS *Queen Mary* and were treated to grandiose dinners, followed by cigars and dinner mints served on silver trays with the Churchill family coat of arms. Nevertheless, Churchill and his staff followed strict routines and kept a grueling schedule on board, which included making plans for aerial offensives and invasions against Hitler. Churchill also insisted that the lifeboat that was assigned to him would be fitted with a .303 machine gun so that he could, as he himself put it, "resist capture at all costs." Along on board with Churchill on that trip, and also headed for the United States, had been five thousand German prisoners of war.

In order to handle the large number of people aboard on a troop crossing, the elegant first-class dining room had been converted into a twenty-four-hour mess hall. It could offer each passenger only one sitting a day to provide everyone a meal. Eating and sleeping schedules had to be rotated around the clock in order to give everyone a turn. At mealtime, June and Hazel and the other nurses had to wait their turn along with everyone else on board and were assigned to their queue in the mess hall.

"Your turn, girls." A young corpsman waved them on. "Remember, twenty minutes until the next seating begins."

"What do you think it'll be today?" June asked.

"Rice and beans," Hazel guessed, and she was right. Due to the restricted storage space on board, the meals consisted mainly of rice and beans. To hold them for the rest of the day, the passengers received small packages containing snacks and a drink.

More than two thousand stateroom doors had been removed in order to install tiers of wooden bunks and rows of canvas hammocks for the troops to sleep in. The *Queen Mary's* fancy shops and boutiques had been turned into quarters for the military officers. Gone were the plush carpets, art deco furnishings, and the crystal, china, and silverware, which had all been put in storage somewhere along the Hudson River. All of the elegance was stripped away. The RMS *Queen Mary* had been transformed into "the GI-shuttle." During the early part of the war, the three largest liners in the world, the *Queen Mary*, the *Queen Elizabeth*, and the *Normandie*, sat idle in port. Finally, the Allied commanders decided that all three ships could be used as troopships. (*Normandie* was destroyed by fire during her troopship conversion.)

On this voyage in early June of 1943, the *Gray Ghost* continued her duty as a GI troopship. At the time, the transformation of the RMS *Queen Mary* into the *Gray Ghost* was not generally known. As June walked up the enclosed gangway and onto the Promenade deck on that first day, she, along with everyone else who came aboard, had been astonished at the size of the ship that was to transport them across the Atlantic. And when they found out that they were really on the *Queen Mary*, they had hardly been able to believe it.

During the rest of the war, the *Gray Ghost* was to make transatlantic shuttles with almost the same frequency as in her prewar days of civilian passenger travel. Whiling away the time on board during the six-day crossing—which, due to the zigzagging, was slower than usual—the troops and medical staff passed the time by playing cards, watching films, and reading books, as well as partaking in daily lifeboat and abandon-ship drills, exercises, and training lectures. There was no privacy to be had. Wherever June went people stood or sat or walked around or lay in their bunks fast asleep, taking their turns in all activities. One place of solace and quietude existed on board: the Catholic, Protestant, and Jewish chapels, which were still available for prayer, and June, a devout Catholic, went to chapel regularly.

When the ship was nearing Europe, the passengers began to hear and see planes in the skies. There were some anxious moments on board then, but the *Gray Ghost* was not attacked. Less than a week earlier, when they boarded, June had felt almost exuberant, as if starting out on a great adventure. Now, the realization of the nightmare that they were racing toward gave her chills. Soon, they would be in the war zone.

Finally in sight of land, the *Ghost* made her way between the land masses of Ireland and Scotland, passing the northern coast of Ireland and turning southward into the North Channel, then turning up into the Firth of Clyde. After passing by Arran Isle, they finally arrived at Gourock Harbor in Scotland, a little northwest of Glasgow. There the passengers collected their scant belongings and stepped onto solid ground again. There had been no time to issue uniforms to the nurses, who still wore civilian clothes, by now uncomfortably dingy. The nurses carried only small valises, crammed with the most basic necessities.

In Gourock, the enlisted men were sent ahead of the hospital personnel, who were to follow afterward. On arrival in nearby Glasgow, the 120th Station unit proceeded by train southward to England. The countryside in Scotland was beautiful, and June, being of Scottish ancestry, felt a sudden rush of pride. Along the way, she tried to picture her ancestors living somewhere in the Scottish hillside, which soon turned into an undulating, green landscape. When they got further south, into the cities of England, the green landscape suddenly changed into a depressing, brown miasma.

June's group was to travel, first by train, then in army convoys of Forty-and-Eight trucks, until their arrival at a staging area at the Lilford Estate in Northamptonshire. Expecting large numbers of injured soldiers from upcoming invasions, the order for June's unit, and the many other groups that followed, was to set up *station hospitals* on various sites in England. As she sat in the train, traversing the dank, brown countryside, June wondered what lay ahead.

June was determined to shape her own future, to be as strong and stubborn as Eleanor Roosevelt, to be compassionate, and to serve others. June knew she was headed toward the hardship and pain that comes with war. After the war, she thought—when she returned home one day—she wanted stability, happiness and a purpose in life, and she knew already that nursing would be the key to fulfilling all her wishes.

# CHAPTER TWO

# JUNE'S EARLY LIFE

1920: Mexican Revolution ends. Greece restores its monarchy.

1921: Adolf Hitler becomes Fuehrer of the Nazi Party.

1925: Hitler's Mein Kampf is published.

1928: Discovery of penicillin by Alexander Fleming.

1929: Wall Street crash. The beginning of the Great Depression.

1932: Franklin D. Roosevelt elected President of the United States.

1934: Hitler becomes Fuehrer of Germany.

1935: The Dustbowl "Black Sunday."

1936: Hoover Dam is completed. Arab revolt in Palestine against the British begins to oppose Jewish immigration.

1937: Beginning of World War II in the Far East. The Golden Gate Bridge opens. The Buchenwald Concentration Camp opens. Amelia Earhart's Plane goes missing.

1938: Kristallnacht in Germany. Time Magazine names Adolf Hitler Man of the Year.

1939: Nazi invasion of Poland triggers the beginning of World War II in Europe.

June Elizabeth Houghton, daughter to George and Florence Houghton, was born on June 1, 1920, in Minneapolis, Minnesota. June's mother, Florence, born Flora Ann Quealy, had been born in the same bed in that same house. June's maternal grandparents were immigrants: her grandfather, Patrick James Quealy had come from County Clare, Ireland, and her grandmother, Teresa McIntosh (named after St. Teresa) was from Scotland.

June's father, George Houghton, came from Middleton, Massachusetts. George had been on a submarine in World War I, and on his return to the United States worked as mechanical engineer with the Brockton Transport Co. in Massachusetts. During the depression, he joined the American Legion in a strike in Detroit, which cost him his job. He then went to work for the Works Progress Administration, earning $12.00 a week. Later he was promoted to a better position in the WPA Red Cross section and got a raise to $15.00 per week. George was a restless man and started a lifelong habit of traveling the country in search of a better job. One day he ended up in Minnesota, and there he found himself a wife, Florence.

While June was still an infant, George got restless again and left Florence, June, and June's four-year-old brother, Warren, and moved back east to Brockton, Massachusetts.

*June, about three years old, in Minneapolis, Minnesota.*

When June was six, her mother died of tuberculosis. George and Florence had been divorced by then, and the children's grandmother in Minnesota took them in.

Four years later, when June was ten, her grandmother died. The children were now orphans, with nowhere to go. A woman named Edna, who with her husband had been close friends of June's parents, sent a letter to George in Massachusetts and told him to come and get his children, threatening that they would otherwise be left in an orphanage in state custody. By the time George got back to Minneapolis, June and Warren had already been placed in a foster home. Remembering that time, more than eighty years later, still makes June cry. Left with total strangers, she had been frightened and overwhelmed by a feeling of loneliness and of missing her mother and grandmother. What had saved her was her brother Warren, already at fourteen a steadfast and calming presence, being there with her.

On his arrival in Minneapolis, George had to go to court in order to get custody of the children. One of the complications was that Florence had changed her own and the children's last names from Houghton to her maiden name, Quealy. With all the paperwork finally taken care of, George went to gather up his children. On the day he came to get them, June did not know him, never even having seen a picture of him. To her, what was happening seemed just the beginning of another frightening time, suddenly traveling across the country to a faraway place that she did not know, Brockton, Massachusetts. Would things get better or worse now? she wondered.

It was the year after the crash on Wall Street. Times were hard, and jobs were few and paid little. Eventually, George managed to get a good job and had them boarded with a family from Nova Scotia with four children of their own.

They lived in Massachusetts until June was sixteen, when her parents' old friend Edna suddenly turned up on a visit to Boston. Her husband had just died—of tuberculosis, just as June's mother had. The visit turned into a long stay, as Edna moved in with them, sharing June's bedroom. June was by then a freshman at Brockton High, enjoying the stability of high school and friends. However, later that summer, George, who by now had saved up some money, decided to move westward again, this time to California. He packed Edna and the children into a big van he had just bought, and June and Warren were among the first children to go across country in a van. June had come to feel at home in Massachusetts and was now torn between sadness at losing her school friends and excitement at going back west, to a place she had so long thought of as home.

When they finally arrived in Idaho, June's brother, Warren, suddenly decided to return to Massachusetts on his own and join a CCC (Civilian Conservation Corps) camp for young people up in Maine, a program started by Roosevelt during the Depression. June ached at seeing him go, Warren having been the only stable connection in her life. June and her father and Edna continued on and eventually arrived in Pocatello, Idaho, a small town known as "the Gateway to the Northwest." It was an old town built by pioneers, gold miners, and prospectors. Driving down the wide main street, lined by buildings straight out of a Wild West movie, June thought, they could see snow covered mountains in the distance. George stopped suddenly and left June sitting on a bench outside Town Hall, telling her to wait there while he and Edna went inside.

"Well June," her father said when they came back out, "now you have a mother again." The two had just gotten married, and June stood gaping at the couple. She liked Edna, and as soon as she caught her breath, she suddenly felt more at ease. There was one drawback: with Edna finally sharing George's bed, June now had to sleep alone, and the first few nights left her feeling cold.

George drove them far up into the mountains of Idaho. Edna owned a cabin up in the hills where they spent some time, but they eventually ended up living in a small, rural place without schools, stores, or close neighbors.

"But Dad," June insisted, "I want to go to school!"

"Sorry girl, that's impossible. You'd have to go down to McCall and board there, and that I can't afford."

One day he had business in McCall, and June was allowed to tag along. While her father took care of his business, June walked around in the town and asked people if they needed a girl to help out, and, *miraculously*, she thought, found a family. In exchange for room and board, she would take care of the three children. That way she was finally able to go back to school, starting out again as a freshman. The biology teacher in the school was elated that June wanted to take biology, as he needed three students in order to teach a class, and June had just become the third student.

Back in those days, McCall was a small town with no sidewalks. It has grown since then and has become quite a popular resort area. Trying to settle in, June had barely gotten to know her schoolmates before George decided to go back to his original plan to move all the way to California. They packed up again, and away they went. George drove them through Salt Lake City in Utah and continued into Nevada. They passed through Las Vegas, which then was just a country road edged with shacks. Apparently some gambling was going on in some of the shacks, but George didn't stop. Instead, he took June and Edna on a long side trip to the Grand Canyon before turning back and getting onto Route 66, which was then also called the Lincoln Highway, toward Los Angeles. George made one last side trip, this time up to San Francisco, no doubt to impress his, by then, travel-weary daughter by showing her the newly opened Golden Gate Bridge.

The day they arrived in Glendale, outside Los Angeles and near Burbank, June thought that this venture was to go from the ridiculous to the sublime. Here, instead of the small rural school in McCall, she got to go to the John Marshall High School, and right on the corner across from the high school was the beginning of Walt Disney Studios—and Disney's nephew Charles was in June's class. That was the sublime part. However, the school was so huge that she felt lost in it.

"Well, then, if that's the case," George said, "we'll just move back to New England." And without further ado, they packed up again, and headed east.

When they arrived in Massachusetts, it was springtime, and June went back to Brockton High, the school where she had originally started out her freshman year. Now, finally, she was a sophomore. After finishing at the CCC camp, Warren had joined the Merchant Marines, serving on the USS *Edwards*. When he returned from his tour, he brought June a beautiful oriental silk robe with a dragon on the back, which June wrapped herself in whenever she felt lonely. She was happy to have everyone together again and prayed that she would be able to stay and graduate, when, suddenly, ever on the move, George decided to move back to California again. This time he was leaving the children behind. George and Edna left for the West, and June and her brother were on their own.

June and Warren were suddenly forced to set up house-keeping together in Massachusetts. By now, Warren was twenty-one and June was seventeen, and they had to remain "very inconspicuous," Warren said, "or else we might be open to criticism." Consequently, June was never allowed to have visitors—she and her brother had to really *obey the rules of the time.* And that was the way she finished her junior and senior years at Brockton High.

Ever since she was a girl, June had dreamed of becoming a nurse, and after graduation she applied to nursing school at Cambridge City Hospital, praying she would be accepted. She was filled with both pride and gratitude when she got word—especially since, in those days, the students who were accepted got to live in the nurses' home, which meant Warren didn't have to shoulder the responsibility for her any longer. However, her brother still insisted on paying for her uniforms and everything else she needed. For three years, Warren came every Thursday to visit and support her with both funds and encouragement, and to make sure she was managing. When June thinks about how wonderful her brother was, it still makes her cry. In 1940, Warren was back in the service, this time the air force. About to be sent to the Pacific, he had just taken an Officer Candidate exam, and entering the Candidate School kept him from being sent off. Warren remained in the service in the United States, where he continued looking after his sister. On June's twenty-first birthday, he arrived at the Cambridge City Hospital with a fancy birthday cake in a box. They each had a slice, sitting in front of the hospital crematorium, before June had to go back to class.

*June and Warren outside Cambridge City Hospital on June's twenty-first birthday*

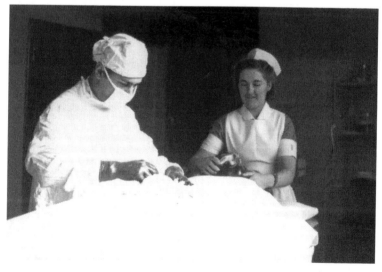

*June and Dr. Fiumara at Cambridge City Hospital in 1941*

June took her State Boards of Nursing exams in October of 1942 and received her RN, Registered Nurse degree, in January of '43. During this time, she also worked in the Cahill House delivery room at the Cambridge City Hospital.

She decided to take a short leave of absence to go visit her father in California, whom she now hadn't seen for six years. She used some of the money she had managed to save up out of Warren's generous allowance and bought a train ticket. Getting on the train, June felt she was in heaven. She didn't have a berth, but she did have a coach seat, and every day she had clean towels and a face cloth, and there was a beautiful bathroom where she could wash up and get into her clothes. The dining rooms were fabulous, the tables set with linen tablecloths and napkins. June happily existed on one meal a day. The trip took five days, and then she was back again in California. She arrived there at the end of January and stayed until the end of April. Toward the end she applied for work in a local hospital, where she worked for a single day. She had been put in a ward full of raucous and fresh male patients, who taunted the pretty, young girl fiendishly. June was shocked and returned to Massachusetts, where she went back to work in the Cahill House delivery room.

On May 26, 1943, June enlisted in the army and began her service in the AANC, the Army Auxiliary Nursing Corps, which later turned into the full-fledged ANC. On May 27, June reported at Camp Edwards in Massachusetts. After one week there, she went to Fort Dix in New York, and by early June, she was on the high seas, on her way into the unknown.

# CHAPTER THREE

# SOUTH DEPARTMENT, BOSTON CITY HOSPITAL

August 24, 1939: Roosevelt asks Hitler and Poland to avoid war.

September 3, 1939: Great Britain declares war on Germany.

May, 1940: Auschwitz concentration camp opens.

May 11, 1940: Churchill in historic address tells Britain the war means blood, sweat, tears.

September 7, 1940—May 10, 1941: The London Blitz.

November 6, 1940: Roosevelt reelected, wins thirty-eight states to Willkie's ten.

December 7, 1940: Joseph P. Kennedy resigns as Ambassador to England.

December 7, 1941: Japan attacks Pearl Harbor, Philippines, Guam, forcing United States into war.

December 8, 1941: Congress votes war 470–1; Britain declares war on Japan.

January of 1941: The US Army has Rommel on the run in Africa. The Afrika Corps is retreating, streaking through Tripoli. MacArthur stops the Japanese on New Guinea and is building a base in Australia. The US Navy is in the Pacific. At home, war bonds are sold, scrap metal drives held. The Manhattan Project at Oak Ridge begins.

January 20, 1942: Wannsee Conference held, resulting in Hitler's "Final Solution": thirty concentration and extermination camps.

After the crossing on the *Gray Ghost*, ensconced on the packed train through Scotland and England, June shared memories with her friends as they sat looking out at the countryside. They were in England now, having left the Scottish hillsides. It was raining, and the raindrops were running down the dirty train windows; the world outside was a study in brown. Depressed at the sight, the girls sat back and listened to June.

In 1939, after graduating from High School, June had gone to Cambridge City Hospital to begin her three-year study in nursing, which included an affiliation at the South Department. She soon learned that this institution was quite different from an ordinary hospital.

"The South Department was the part of Boston City Hospital that was confined to communicable diseases, and it was over in South Boston," June began, thinking back. "That branch of the hospital was the center for all contagion that went on in and around Boston and the surrounding areas, and it had separate wards, you see, each ward for one type of infection. Take mumps, for instance, there'd be one confined area that would be all mumps cases; there would be a confined area of scarlet fever; there'd be a large area that contained the iron lung—because the iron lung was so big—that was used for polio. We had also something called *wards of cubicle*, and each cubicle would contain a different type of communicable disease. The precautionary measures were different when you worked in that area because each cubicle was a different type of disease; therefore you had to wash your hands carefully and soak them in Lysol, and then you had to don coverings over your uniform, and then a mask, and only then could you go into that cubicle. When you finished taking care of the patient and left the cubicle, you had to go through the same process again, in reverse."

"What kinds of diseases were you dealing with, then? Hazel asked.

"Oh, most of the patients at South were children with diphtheria, typhoid, polio, and all those very serious types of diseases that attacked the throat and swallowing mechanisms. Those children had to be *intubated*. That was a new method, and if the intubation didn't work, then they would have to do a tracheotomy—which was the old way, you know. What the intubation was, they would put a stainless steel tool down the patient's throat to open it up or to clear it to get the air through—but then, if the intubation didn't work, they would quickly have to do a tracheotomy. It was always a rush thing, time was of the essence. Only if you were very lucky could a tracheotomy be closed at another time, but for most of the survivors they ended up being permanent in order for the person to be able to breathe right, so the intubation method was a great improvement."

The listeners looked out the train window at the desolate landscape before returning their attention to the twenty-three-year old lecturer. June smiled patiently, and continued where she left off.

"Now, the iron lung department...some of the people there didn't survive too long. Some would recover from polio, but would remain partially paralyzed. We had this one woman, named Celia, who could only move one index finger. She could blink her eyes, she could talk, and she could read, and the two doctors who were in charge of South Department, I forget the name of one of them, but the other one I remember because it was different—his name was Dr. Prizer—well, they devised a mechanism for Celia to be able to flip pages in a book with her one index finger. We would clip the pages back, leaving twenty-five pages loose, which meant she could read fifty.

"When you worked in South Department," she continued, "you worked there for three months as an affiliate student, from all different hospitals. Every one of us who affiliated there had to take our turn taking care of Celia because her care was so complete that it taught you how to take care of a person who is totally immobilized. And she never had a bedsore, never a heel sore, which is something you commonly get with someone who is completely bedridden, but because of the care we were taught to give her and the massage that we had to do, she never had any of those problems."

"She had polio?" Nellie asked. "Most of the iron lung patients had polio, right?"

"She had polio, yes. After a while, she had gained enough knowledge herself that she knew how to gasp air into her lungs so that she could stay out of the iron lung for a while, with somebody taking care of her standing beside her the whole time. The type of nursing we did was so important because Celia also didn't have to have a catheter to drain off urine. We were taught how to press down on her bladder to make her void. And of course you'd have to give her a drink of water to institute it. Also, we didn't really have to give her daily enemas because we were taught how to manipulate the rectal area. You might have to give her an enema once a month to clear the bowel out. We, as I say, had a very extensive nursing care at South Department. What a place that was. It was located at a separate site, away from Boston City Hospital, you know."

"So, at the end of the day, when you left, where did you go? Were you staying in the nurse's home or with your brother then?" asked Nellie.

"Oh, no, you had to live at South," June laughed. "And you had to have clearance to get in and out, every time, as a young, student nurse. Just anybody couldn't go in and out all the time because of the communicable diseases that could be spread. If you wanted to go home on a pass, you had to have permission to leave and get clearance to go out of the building, but generally you were so tired you didn't really want to go anywhere. If you had a day off, you might ask for permission to leave, but most of the time your hands were in such terrible condition from dipping them into the Lysol, and in some areas into...dichloride of mercury, I think it was, barrels of it. And evidently the precautionary measures we were taught to be able to take care of all this type of disease must have been very thorough because this method had a marvelous record of nontransferable germs."

"So, you had to share rooms, or did you have a room of your own there? And what about food?"

"Oh, we were very well fed. In my area, there were four of us from Cambridge City Hospital. Next to us were four more, and then across, there were four from Cambridge Mount Auburn, and next to them there were four from Maine General, up in Maine. So it really had quite a cross section of people coming to learn about communicable diseases because it was such a special center."

"So when was this? Just before you enlisted?"

"No, it was at the end of forty-one. I was there on Pearl Harbor Day. And we were all put on the alert at that time because the hospital administration thought we were being invaded, so none of us got to go anyplace, no matter what. Well…I remember it was near Christmastime, yes, and because we were put on the alert, we could none of us get home for Christmas. Oh, how I missed Warren! He was still helping me out, you know. I don't know how I'd ever get by without him. But anyway, afterward I went back to Cambridge City Hospital to finish my time there.

"Oh, one of the things I remember from Cambridge City Hospital was something that happened there once in the middle of the night. We had a patient named Bill, who had been hit by a car. Apart from the injuries he had, he was half drunk and not making much sense. During the night I worried about him, and so I decided to go and check on him with my friend Gracie, a black girl. It was dark in the patient's room, and we had to carry flashlights. I remember I couldn't see Gracie walking in front of me, except for the white cap and apron-strings moving. We shined our flashlights on Bill, and his face was blown up like a balloon. To touch his skin was like touching a sponge full of air. 'Oh, it's crepitus,' I said. We put in an emergency call, and the doctor came immediately. It turned out that Bill, with all his other injuries, had received a fractured trachea in the accident, and now they had to do a tracheotomy, which saved his life. I got a commendation for going to check on him and making the emergency call. Later, when Bill recovered, he actually started helping out in the wards and was there for a long while. I wonder what happened to him. He was so nice, and we learned to understand his speech after a while, when he remembered to press a finger on his throat to speak. Of course, his voice was quite strange. Anyway, I finished my affiliation at CCH in February of forty-two."

By now, Grace (her name often got June to think about Gracie, her constant companion back at Cambridge City Hospital, and wonder how Gracie was doing) was leaning back in her seat, eyes half shut. None of the friends had slept well during the long ocean voyage, and they were happy to be on dry land, away from the threat of submarines on the open sea.

In the eighteen-forties and -fifties, Boston, one of the debarkation points when famine in Europe brought immigrants with cholera and other infectious diseases to the United States, had one major hospital, and that was the Massachusetts General Hospital, which was fast becoming overcrowded. Ships' passengers were not detained to be checked at the Deer Island Hospital, the city's quarantine hospital, and disease soon became rampant throughout the city. With the large waves of immigrants, most of them Irish, arriving on "coffin ships," many of them dying on the way over, the poor were being sent off unchecked into the reeking "Paddyvilles" and "Mick Alleys" of Boston. These were the first urban slums of America, often with thirty or forty people packed into small spaces in primitive shacks. In these areas there were constant problems with backed-up drains, numerous families having to share a toilet, and sometimes one sink for a whole tenement. In some places, one outhouse served the whole neighborhood. Cholera, small-pox, and tuberculosis were common.

The city then opened a building on Fort Hill, near the waterfront, where the Fort Hill Hospital was created to serve destitute patients with cholera—including those who had been refused admittance to the overcrowded Massachusetts General. Fort Hill Hospital proved to be highly effective, and soon a bequest by a grateful patient named Elisha Goodnow led to the creation of the Boston City Hospital.

Boston City Hospital opened in 1864. Officials under-stood the need for separate buildings in order to treat each con-tagious disease, and a smallpox hospital was constructed on the grounds. Smallpox was, at the time, more feared than cholera, diphtheria, scarlet fever, measles, and other infectious diseas-es. Only a few years later, the Boston City Hospital became so overcrowded that tents had to be erected in the yard for extra wards. In the next few years, new surgical and medical build-ings were erected.

In 1895, the Boston City Hospital opened the new South Department—the first entirely separate hospital for the treat-ment of infectious diseases in the United States—headed by Dr. John McCollom, who was soon named physician-in-chief. The South Department was built on a large site in South Boston. Dr. McCollom was one of the first physicians in the United States to use diphtheria antitoxin. He also adopted Dr. Joseph O'Dwyer's approach to airway management of diphtheria patients by performing tracheal *intubation* rather than tracheotomy. Dr. Edwin Place, who followed him, held the same belief and continued this practice.

The South Department started out with seven buildings: administration, east pavilion and west pavilion, gate-lodge, domestic, laundry, and the home for nurses. Aside from the wards being purposely exposed to the open air on four sides, there were steam sterilizers for disinfecting mattresses and other articles that could not be disinfected by boiling, as well as a special crematory for burning garbage and refuse.

Each two-story building, divided by open-air transverse corridors, was separated into four completely isolated wards on each floor. All buildings were arranged so that the sunlight would enter freely.

In 1920, a small toddler named John Fitzgerald Kennedy had developed scarlet fever. The hospital in Brookline, where the family lived at the time, did not admit patients with contagious diseases. Rose Kennedy worried that the other three children, Joe, Rosemary, and the newborn baby Kathleen, would also come down with the fever. After learning of the reputation of Dr. Edwin Place, Rose became determined to have her child taken to South Department, and young John Kennedy was finally admitted (after some help from "Honey Fitz," John Francis Fitzgerald, Rose Kennedy's maternal grandfather and former Boston mayor).

Joseph Kennedy "vividly recalled the distressing experience of leaving his two-and-a-half-year-old son in the small, sterile room, which doctors, nurses, and attendants could enter only after thoroughly scrubbing their hands and putting on a specially disinfected gown." Upset by the experience, Joseph went to church to pray for Jack's recovery every morning, promising, "If Jack is spared, I will give half of my money to charity." Every afternoon, he left his office early and journeyed to the hospital, where he sat for long periods on the edge of his boy's bed. For three months the toddler John Kennedy received the skilled medical care at South Department before being returned to his home in good health.

Joseph Kennedy later wrote to Dr. Place to thank him:

I would indeed be an ingrate if I let this chance pass by without telling you how much I appreciate your wonderful work for Jack during his recent illness. I had never experienced any very serious sickness in my family previous to Jack's, and I realized what an effect such a happening could possibly have on me. During the darkest days I felt that nothing else mattered except his recovery, and you must have some notion of what the gratitude of a parent can be to have his boy returned in the wonderful shape that Jack seems to be now.

Joseph Kennedy fulfilled his pledge to God by giving a check to the Guild of St. Apollonia, an organization of Catholic dentists, to provide dental care to children in Catholic schools. The amount of the check was $3,750, which, according to Rose, was exactly half of his fortune at that time.

Dr. Place laid great stress on the need for isolation for scarlet fever and of disinfecting everything that had been exposed to infection from the patients. The largest part of deaths following scarlet fever is due to pneumonia. The main thing in saving scarlet fever patients, therefore, was to see that they don't get pneumonia, or that its severity was minimized by the high quality nursing care developed at South Department.

*Since that day, the South Department has been torn down. Ironically, it was recently announced that a bill has passed legislation to build, or house, a research center in South Boston for the study of communicable diseases.*

# CHAPTER FOUR

# LILFORD ESTATE, NORTHAMPTONSHIRE

April 19, 1943: Reports tell of Nazi annihilation of 2,000 European Jews by gas chamber, mass execution.

May 11, 1943: The Trident Conference between the United States and Britain begins. Roosevelt and Churchill decide to delay the Allied invasion of France and in its place plan the Allied invasion of Italy.

May 16, 1943: German troops crush the last resistance of the Warsaw Ghetto Uprising and kill thousands of Jews. The rest are sent to the Treblinka concentration camp to die.

June 2, 1943: Leslie Howard lost in a passenger plane shot down by Nazis.

June 6th 1943: The Allied D-Day landings in the North of France eventually render the French-German U-boat bases inoperable.

The great film star Leslie Howard had been shot down while Lt. June Houghton and the soldiers and nurses aboard the *Gray Ghost* had made it safely, zigzagging across the Atlantic, and could breathe more easily now that they were on British soil. But now the terrible tidings of what was happening to the Jews were spreading. What June and the other nurses heard defied all belief. How could it be true? The war was endlessly expanding, it seemed. Was there any person on earth not touched by it? Anywhere that was safe? Here in England, they began to feel exposed to something they had not quite understood while living in the distant United States.

*Lilford Hall, Northamptonshire*

The 120th Station unit finally arrived at Lilford Hall, a stately castle situated south of Oundle in Northamptonshire in the center of England. The Lilford Estate was surrounded by acres of fields and woods. Lilford Park had been turned over for military and hospital use by Lord Lilford, who still lived in a wing of the castle. The park was famous for its beautiful rose garden. During a brief excursion into the garden, the heady, sun-warmed scent of roses followed June along the path. It was only when she turned and saw in the background the large area that was now occupied by the military—the rows of tents, the vehicles, and the dust raised by the workers—that she remembered what they were there for. June managed to take a quick snapshot of a young man among the military unit, Sgt. Robert Gardner, the A&D (admission and discharge) officer of the 120th Station Hospital, before hurrying back to the station, where they all soon found out that this was no time to smell the roses.

Throughout England, American soldiers, nurses, and corpsmen were arriving to set up station hospitals in the large, open fields of major estates. Everyone, including the medical staff, had to pitch in to get the stations set up and in order before patients would begin to arrive. At this line of *echelon*, or level of command, they weren't quite as well equipped with personnel as the receiving stations were.

They soon learned the order in which the taking care of wounded soldiers was to go: the injured were taken from the battlefield and brought to the *First Aid Receiving*. Next in order were the *Field Hospitals*. Following them were the *Station Hospitals*. Last in order were the *General Hospitals*, which were located inland, and which were also the ones that took care of the most severely wounded patients, sending many them to the United States.

The mission of the medical department was to give excellent medical care and, whenever possible, return the soldier to the field. *"Conserve the Fighting Strength"* was the motto.

The receiving stations did triage and sent the very gravest cases right to the general hospital. Other patients—called "bandages" and other nicknames—would go to treatment in the field hospital. When the less seriously wounded field hospital patients had recovered sufficiently, they would be returned directly to the battlefield. The more seriously injured soldiers who had to be operated on, or who had fractured bones, or bones to be realigned, went to the station hospitals. From there, if their case became grave, they were sent to the general hospital. The General hospital staff would do what they could, but if the case was too difficult even for them, or if they didn't have the resources, the patient would be sent to the United States for care.

# CHAPTER FIVE

# LONDON

June 17, 1943: Allies bomb Sicily and the Italian mainland, as signs increase of a forthcoming invasion.

June 22, 1943: Army quells Detroit race riots, twenty-three dead.

June 24, 1943: Continuing attacks against the Ruhr Valley, resulting in large evacuations of German civilians from the area.

July 1, 1943: The US government begins directly withholding income tax from wages.

A few days after their arrival at the Lilford Estate, the chief nurse made it known that she needed three nurses to go to London to pick up medications.

"This is how we do it: you draw straws, and that will decide who gets to go," she said, holding out her hand for them to pull a straw.

June was one of the lucky ones, along with Marion and Jody, and these three were sent off on a train into London, with the paperwork safely stowed in a leather briefcase.

They were to stay at the residence of United States Ambassador Anthony Joseph Drexel Biddle, Jr., on Charles Street in London, near Groveland Square. Ambassador Biddle was also commissioned to the governments-in-exile of Belgium, Czechoslovakia, Greece, Luxembourg, the Netherlands, Norway, and Yugoslavia. The residence had been turned over for war-time use as a Red Cross office as well as for the housing of American nurses. On their arrival in London, June and her companions had to go immediately and sign in with the embassy. When they were logged in at the residence, they were sternly told that every time they went in or out they had to report at the desk. Also, they were advised, they must be back and signed in by eleven o'clock at night.

Their first order of business was to get the medications. The issuing of drugs was supervised by the American Embassy staff. Armed with the leather bag, the three nurses waited in line at the embassy. After properly identifying themselves and turning all the paperwork over to the pharmacist, there was another long wait. Ultimately, when the pharmacist showed up with all that was requested, there was a substantial package for each of them to carry back to their unit.

"I wonder what's in the packages," June said, hefting one.

"Well, sulfa, of course," Marion figured.

Until it was time to go back to Lilford, they stored the boxes in a closet in their room at the Biddle House.

"Let's put a blanket over them to hide them," June said. They had begun to realize that this errand carried a lot of responsibility for young girls of twenty-two or twenty-three, but now, relieved, they had the medicine safely stowed away.

They were impressed with their room at the Biddle House, especially the fancy bathroom. It suddenly reminded June of her rather lavish train trip to visit her father in California. However, there was a fixture in the bathroom that they were curious about.

"What is that thing?" Jody asked, pointing at what looked like a cross between a toilet and a low wash basin. "Is it for washing your feet?" They tested it, but it still seemed a conundrum. They were a bit too shy to ask, and were not to find out until much later what a *bidet* was used for.

They listened to the "wireless" in their room. The wireless was a fancy, polished wooden radio with three knobs: one to turn it on, one for volume, and one for tuning. The sound came out through a cloth-covered area. The programs were limited to the news, which was all very discouraging, and the music of the day. "The Nightingale Sang in Berkeley Square" became an instant favorite, along with "Lili Marlene."

The nurses were shocked at the destruction in some of the neighborhoods they wandered through in the afternoon.

Despite the gas masks, they often sensed an unpleasant odor when a sewage pipe had been hit, and they would quickly scurry around the corner, feeling sorry for the people living in the area.

On their first night in London, the girls went to a movie—only, in their excitement, they'd forgotten all about the blackout. When the movie let out, it was pitch black outside.

"Now, what do we do?" Marion said.

No moon or stars, no street lights, and with the blackout curtains, not a shred of light shining from windows to give them at least an idea of where the sidewalk might be. Not even flashlights were allowed.

"Does anyone remember which direction we came from?" June asked, trying to be calm and sensible, but no one could remember. Reaching out to touch the walls of buildings, trees, or fences as they passed, they proceeded slowly down the street, turning the corner when a row of buildings ended. Suddenly June and Marion found themselves alone. Jody had disappeared. After frantic calling, they were reunited, and then went on more carefully, holding hands.

They wandered around this way, hoping to find some transport back to the Charles Street address. Occasionally they heard voices, and called out to ask if someone could offer them a ride. Once, out of the darkness, they got a response.

"Sorry, no petrol."

A few people tried to help them by pointing them in the right direction, but the girls soon lost the trail again, slowly groping their way through the darkened city blocks. They were scared to death by then and gripped one another's hands tightly.

Finally they came across a taxi driver who took pity on them and said he'd take them back. When they finally arrived at the Biddle House, they had to appear before the Red Cross staff member in charge to sign in and explain what happened. June and her friends had arrived at one-thirty in the morning and were immediately put on report, as they were two and a half hours late. Therefore, they had been listed as AWOL, which would go on their records.

They stayed the rest of that night in their room, as the bombings seemed to be over, but on the following night, they went down to the shelter as soon as they heard the sound of "Moaning Minnie," which was the Londoners' nickname for the air-raid siren. As soon as the siren started, all the cats and dogs in the neighborhood chimed in, howling and mewing for all they were worth. The bombings, when they came, seemed to start at the same time every evening.

The worst bombings, of course, had been during "The Blitz" in 1940 and '41. But Hitler continued his attacks, with these special orders:

> When targets are being selected, preference is to be given to those where attacks are likely to have the greatest possible effect on civilian life. Besides raids on ports and industry, terror attacks of a retaliatory nature are to be carried out against towns other than London. Mine laying is to be scaled down in favor of these attacks. *(Signal from the Fuehrer's headquarters to the Luftwaffe High Command, 14 April 1942.)*

The "Moaning Minnie" alarm lasted for one minute, on a rising and falling note, and the streets were suddenly crowded with people rushing to the shelters. Some people chose to stay at home. The current bombing attacks were nothing like those during the Blitz, but the nurses were not about to take any chances.

"Let's go, hurry up. We'll leave everything here, except remember to take your gas masks!" June said, as they pulled on their coats. They were required to have their gas masks with them at all times and, being in the military, whenever they went outdoors they had to don the masks. During the day they had done a practice run from the Biddle House to the shelter, so they wouldn't get lost again.

When they got down into the shelter, which was located in the underground, or as the British called it, the "tube," people were resting on the floor or on benches along the walls. The walls were covered with propaganda posters. There was generally only one overhead light, which sometimes went off; however, someone always brought candles to light and pass around. Then people sang to keep their spirits up and also to distract the children from hearing the frightening sounds of bombs falling outside. A small area of the shelter was curtained off to serve as the "loo." Behind the curtain was a chamber pot, which was nicknamed the "Gusunder" pot (as it usually "goes under" the bed) and beside it a pile of newspaper torn into "loo paper." The nurses remained in the shelter—but avoided the loo—until the all-clear sounded, and then they hurried back to see whether the American Embassy was still standing. They breathed a sigh of relief when they found that the packages of medicine were still there.

In the midst of all the destruction, they ended up having very little time or desire for old-fashioned sightseeing but managed to get their picture taken standing by "Queen Victoria's Cake," a grand statue commemorating the old queen, outside Buckingham Palace. The statue was made of white marble and looked like a giant wedding cake. Victoria herself, listed as Victoria Regina Imperatrix, was facing east, away from Buckingham Palace. On top of the "cake" were two immense angels, the Angel of Justice and the Angel of Truth. The visit to London was both exciting and sad, June thought, and as they left, she felt sorry for the Londoners who had to live in their beautiful city while watching its destruction.

Later, on the way back to Lilford, June drowsed fitfully on the train, waking up out of nightmares. She twisted and turned in her seat, thinking of her brother Warren and her student nursing days at the South Department in Boston. It all seemed so far away.

## CHAPTER SIX

# LEAVING LILFORD, ON TO BRISTOL

July 1, 1943: MacArthur makes four new landings: New Guinea, Trobriand, Rendova, New Georgia.

July 5, 1943: The Germans enact Operation Citadel – the assault on Kursk.

July 7, 1943: Rocket scientist Wernher von Braun briefs the V-2 rocket to Hitler, who approves the project for top priority.

When the three nurses returned to Lilford, the 120th Station was still awaiting further orders. While they waited, the exhausting training with marches and drills continued daily.

Suddenly the drilling routines intensified, and they sensed that there was going to be a change, wondering what was going to happen. Then, abruptly, they were put on alert, and nobody could leave. Shortly afterward, they were on the move again.

The medical personnel of the 120th Station Hospital had arrived at Lilford Park in Northamptonshire early in the summer of 1943 and stayed there until they were told to pack up and go to another location near Bristol. Later in the year, the USAAF 303rd Station Hospital, which included the 303 Bomb Group, or "Hell's Angels," would set up their station hospital at Lilford Park.

On arrival in Bristol, June and the other nurses were finally issued the AANC nurses uniforms: dark blue jackets, lighter blue skirt, and a long, navy cape. Later, when they became part of the ANC (the Army Nurse Corps), this uniform would be exchanged for one olive drab, along with a white seersucker dress. On duty, they had to wear their uniforms and "dress like women," but when they were off duty, they wore their fatigues.

They had to endure long, exhausting bivouacs and more training sessions during their stay in Bristol, where they were made to practice with their gas masks on, as well as learn how to use the masks and take care of them. The men and women had separate bivouacs, as there was to be no "fraternizing." The nurses marched for hours at a time, wearing gas mask and helmet and carrying heavy equipment.

*120th Station on bivouac outside Bristol*

"Look at us; we're a tired bunch of cookies. Those 'helmuts' are no joke," June complained, pushing at her helmet, while still marching briskly. Hazel, Grace, and Frances were trudging along behind her, too tired to comment, and beginning to wonder what their mission was. Were they ever to be given the opportunity to serve the wounded? They followed the news in the paper, appalled at the headlines about killing and maiming.

On a short furlough between training sessions, Lt. June Houghton, Hazel Hearn, Frances Melle, and Grace Russell got permission for another visit to London. They hurried around to see whatever sights they had time for and had their picture taken in front of 10 Downing Street.

*Hazel, Grace, Frances, and June in front of 10 Downing Street*

In the city, they learned more about the war, listening to the wireless and the people in the street, and reading the billboards at the newsstands. New details coming out about the persecution of Jews and Romanis and other non-Aryans, and about concentration camps, were shocking and hard to believe.

It was madness, the nurses thought. The *Final Solution* must be the ravings of a madman. As the news spread around the world, people began to wonder if it would be possible to stop Hitler.

Returning to Bristol, they finally concluded the training period. Then they continued traveling, first to Bath, and eventually arriving at Tortworth Court in the village of Malmesbury in South Gloucestershire.

# CHAPTER SEVEN

# TORTWORTH COURT, MALMESBURY

July 10, 1943: Allies invade Sicily. Operation Husky is launched.

July 25, 1943: Mussolini deposed, King and Pietro Badoglio rule Italy.

August 2, 1943: John F. Kennedy's PT-109 rammed in two and sunk off the Solomon Islands.

August 15, 1943: Allies land in South France.

August 24, 1943: The Operation Gomorrah firestorm bombing of Hamburg begins. It is the heaviest assault in the history of aerial assault at the time. Paris freed by US and French troops; Marseilles, Grenoble fall.

*Nellie, Sylvia, and Tony, Tortworth Court*

ortworth Court was a mansion in Tudor style and, like the Lilford Estate, surrounded by great open areas and parks, including an extensive arboretum. The setup was similar at all the station hospitals. Quonset huts and tents had to be erected. Masses of tents and Quonset huts were soon lined up and were to be inspected daily. There were large tents for the hospital wards and small, square ones for the enlisted men and hospital staff. Enlisted men and nurses were to live in separate areas, in tents set up in groups of different configurations. The enlisted men's tents were placed in straight lines, the nurses' in compact groups. All tents used by the 120th Station Hospital could be put up and taken down quickly.

*Tents where enlisted men or nurses lived*

Some of the big Quonset huts held surgeries; some held kitchens for patients; others were used as storage for food and for general supplies. A separate area held the long, white tents of the wards. Each of the smaller tents, just a little larger than a pup tent, had to accommodate four nurses or four enlisted men. Inside each of these tents was a small potbellied stove to keep the occupants warm. The nurses would brew their coffee there, too, in a big pot on top of the stove. Of course, the "coffee" was in reality *chicory*, made from the ground and roasted root of chicory, the wartime substitute in Europe. June and the other nurses imagined that sitting in the tent by the stove during the winter might be quite cozy.

The kitchen in the mess tent was supervised by the hospital dietician. The Nurses' Mess was separate from the Enlisted Men's and the Officers' Mess. Food was delivered by a quartermaster depot, and vegetables arrived every other week, along with whatever fruits and juices that were issued.

There were other important shacks and huts to construct. Latrines and ablution huts to be used for bathing had to be built. The women joined other groups at hard labor around the camp. They worked in fatigues, raising tents and digging in the stony soil right alongside the men.

"You can't tell one from the other," June said to Hazel, laughing.

"Sure you can," Hazel retorted, "they've got bigger shovels."

*Alice, Sylvia, and Nellie in fatigues*

There were trenches to dig—they even had to dig latrine trenches, as there were no facilities on the grounds. It was common around the station hospitals in England during the war for farmers to come and collect the sludge, which they would then use to fertilize their fields. Other refuse, such as from the hospital kitchens, was collected by civilian contractors, and trash was collected and dumped at nearby community dumps.

When the nurses were done digging, they inspected the latrines in silence.

"Well, better than the *loo* in the *tube* at least," June said.

*June, Marie, and Mary Ellen outside ablution hut, ready to take a shower*

The nurses had to learn the use of the "Lyster bag," a large, canvas bag that held water from wells or other water sources. The water in the bag had to be purified before drinking, either by using liquid chlorine, a method developed by Major Carl Rogers Darnell, or by a solution of calcium hypochlorite, the second method developed by Major William Lyster, who gave the common name to the bag. The Lyster bag was used by ground forces in the field as well as in camps and on medical stations, and could be hung from a convenient tree or post. The water was doled out from several spigots at the bottom of the bag. The water from the Lyster bag was drawn for cooking, medical use, showers, and other needs. For kitchen use, one bag was issued for every hundred persons.

*Learning how to purify water using Lyster bag*

June and a couple of other nurses carried the bag and supplies over to a clean area to start the process. June read the instructions aloud.

"First we have to clean the bag. We have to use this hypochlorite ampoule and dissolve it in water."

When it was cleaned, they hung the thirty-six-gallon bag from the branch of a tree and filled it with water up to a mark four inches from the top.

"Now we have to dissolve these ampoules of calcium hypochlorite in half a canteen of water, pour it into the Lyster bag, and stir it with a clean stick."

"After half an hour, we flush the six spigots, wait another ten minutes then flush them again before testing the water." They flushed the spigots and sat down and waited, while June read the rest of the instruction aloud.

If the water had a slight blue appearance, it meant that there was enough chlorine concentrated in it and the water was drinkable. If there was no color to the water, it meant that the water was polluted, a fact that had to be immediately reported to the Medical Officer in charge of water supplies. They waited, checking their watches, then drew a cupful.

"Look, it worked! The water's blue," June said, smiling proudly, when the water came out with a slight blue tinge. Lyster bags for common use around the station were hung from tripods made of tent poles, as far away as possible from anything that might cause pollution.

The work routines were tedious and exhausting, and when finished, the nurses had to keep their tents neat; sweep the paths; and do the laundry, which was hung on lines between the tents. There was no need for entertainment or card playing at night, they simply fell into bed and were asleep as soon as the head hit the pillow.

*120th Station, Block G. June in Army Nurse's seersucker dress*

On a rare sunny day, they dragged their blankets out onto the dirt beside the path, and took their short break in the warmth of the sun.

"Oh, look at my legs! Aren't they getting a nice tan?" Nellie asked.

Then, out came the record player. The handle was wound, and the needle guided into the groove of the sturdy 78 record. "The White Cliffs of Dover" with Vera Lynn became a favorite, but "We'll Meet Again" made them all weepy and homesick.

There was a PX (a post exchange) where they could go and read the paper, issued by the Red Cross, to find out news about the war. The PX was like a miniature department store, and the shelves held a small selection of items to fill simple needs such as candy, socks, snacks, cigarettes, toilet articles, and other necessities. Inside there was even a bar with stools, where a beer could be had.

The combined British-Canadian-American invasion of Sicily began on the tenth of July, 1943, under the supreme command of General Dwight D. Eisenhower. There were amphibious and airborne landings by the American Seventh Army under Lt. General George S. Patton. At the Gulf of Gela, north of Syracuse, landings were made by the British Eighth Army under General Montgomery. There was a great loss of life when 69 of the 137 Gliders were unsuccessful and came down in the sea, drowning some 200 men. Only twelve Gliders finally reached their target area. The Highlanders took Catania and Paterno. The historic city of Messina was ravaged by Allied bombs before it fell. By August, *Operation Husky* was termed a success. "The soft underbelly of Europe" had been bared. Now the Mediterranean was wide open for use as a sea route. In the end, it was a costly victory. In this operation, the Allies lost 16,000 men. Of the Axis troops, it was estimated that 164,000 were killed or taken prisoner. June and the other nurses followed the news at the PX, horrified at the loss of life.

The first large contingent of patients at Tortworth came from the African-Italian Campaign. Now there was no free time for the nurses, even for a brief rest during the shift. The schedule was grueling: twelve-hour shifts, either 7:00 a.m. to 7:00 p.m. or 7:00 p.m. to 7:00 a.m., and if they were lucky, a break somewhere in between.

The wounded had been recovered by reconnaissance patrols in enemy territories before being taken to the Field Hospital Receiving Office, processed, and then shipped off to the appropriate level hospital care. When the convoy of ambulances arrived at 120th Station Hospital, there was a triage set up, where the patients were quickly assessed and assigned to the proper wards, depending on the injury or disease.

To further assess the patient's condition, there was a consultation by the patient's bed. The officers of the Medical and Surgical Services would confer, with a nurse taking the notes, and as soon as the treatment necessary had been determined, the patient would be sent to the operating room.

The official ward rounds and medical meetings ran on a regular schedule. There were frequent visits from US and British Army installations, along with special conferences which often included demonstrations and classes on new uses of radiology, on the use of penicillin, and on other new treatments.

*June and three patients from the African-Italian Campaign*

Many of June's patients in this contingent were suffering from flak wounds, chest wounds, broken bones, and injuries suffered in aircraft crashes. These were first taken to the X-ray department. A large number of patients suffered from burns. Abdominal wounds were common, skin graft was often applied, and new surgical methods were introduced. There was a constant flood of patients suffering the loss of blood, and the station had to keep a large blood bank available. In those instances time was always of the essence, and, after crossmatching, June would immediately prepare the patient for transfusion.

The pace was exhausting. The wounds were appalling, one ghastly injury after another. In the hospitals back home there had mostly been an orderly, quiet pace, and time to consider options, but not here, June thought. Everything here was immediate, and urgent.

There were routine types of surgery permitted in station hospitals. Those of a very grave or life threatening nature had to be transferred immediately to the general hospital. At the station, burns were treated with washing and irrigation, followed by treatment with sulfadiazine ointment and occlusive pressure dressing. Sulfa powder and penicillin, which was just coming into use, were also placed in the wound. Wherever available, penicillin rapidly became an efficient treatment of pneumonia, infections, and wounds.

Early in 1944 it had been decided that courses in anesthesiology were urgently needed in the field, and three sessions had been held at 120th Station at Tortworth Court, one each in January, February, and March. It had been an intensive program, though pitifully inadequate, considering the massive scope of the war zone and the pain soldiers had to bear during surgery. However, when compared to services in the field by other nations, the Americans were far ahead, and working hard to improve as rapidly as possible.

Restored to their beds in the ward after an operation, the patients who had been wounded in enemy action would receive their Purple Heart Medal, which was presented to them by the commanding officer.

The 120th Station Hospital had been one of the first places to use penicillin, which was administered as very painful injections. Up until that time, there had been another unusual way among the local people to treat wounds. It was ancient knowledge that honey could be used to dress wounds, due to its special antiseptic properties, and it was said to speed up the healing process. Honey was also used to treat burns and would, according to some, reduce scarring. June had heard that in a nearby Gloucestershire village called Swindon, keeping bees had become a popular side business. In fact, residents keeping bees were granted extra wartime allowances of sugar to keep the bees going through the winter. There had been some cheating, however, when people used the sugar for their private needs, after which the sugar provided to beekeepers was dyed green— a practice that had to be stopped when the honey also turned green.

Tortworth Court, like Lilford, was a handsome and impressive estate. It was situated on a large tract of land, which the Americans were given to use as a hospital area. After asking one of the locals, June learned that the land was not *taken over* by the government; instead, the English were very open about offering the use of their land during the war effort. The American servicemen and medical corps received many invitations to British homes. Villagers were also generous in offering residents of London wartime shelter in the safety of their country homes.

In command of the 120th Station was Dr. Joseph Haas. A first lieutenant in the army during World War I, Dr. Haas had been regimental surgeon with the Eighty-Fourth Division of the 384th Infantry. He was later transferred to the Fourth Division and put in command of the Nineteenth Field Hospital in Europe.

With the outbreak of World War II, Dr. Haas was promoted to colonel and put in command of the 120th Station Hospital, which was to move from Texas to England (and, later in the war, to France and finally to Germany). Dr. Haas was eventually to be awarded the medal of the city of Verdun, the Distinguished Service medal, the Legion of Merit, and the Bronze Star. Dr. Haas had been in command of the 120th since June and her unit arrived and was a doctor well liked and respected by everyone. He was a caring leader, but there were rules to be followed. When Colonel Haas found out that one of his nurses had married a soldier and gotten pregnant, he had to send her home to Fall River, in Massachusetts. June also knew a nice, friendly fellow who was transferred out due to being gay. Those were the rules.

*Col. Haas in chair, Chief Nurse Kay Taylor. Catholic Chaplain Father Andre on left, kneeling*

To meet religious needs, the camp had four chaplains: two Protestant, one Jewish, and then the Catholic chaplain, Father Andre, who was the one June would often seek out. Convalescent patients could attend religious services on Sunday in one of the chapels on the hospital grounds. When bedridden, patients were visited by one of the members of the Chaplain Corps.

Patients who were ambulatory would go to eat in the Patients' Mess instead of in the ward. The convalescing soldiers were also visited by barbers and were allowed the use of other facilities, such as the Post Office and the PX. They could pick up their paychecks at the Detachment of Patients, and even have dental checkups. Before being released from the hospital, either to be sent home or back into the field, the soldiers were given a psychological test to determine their mental condition.

June assisted in cases to do with chest injuries, as chest trauma was her department and the care of any type of chest surgery was her main duty. This included the draining of fluids, the care of bayonet wounds, bullet wounds, and injuries from exploded mines. Most of the chest wounds were from bayonets. If the weapon had been twisted in the wound, it was more serious and more painful and would take longer to heal. June felt at ease caring for her patients in the ward as they were mending after surgery. After a while, she began to enjoy being a bedside nurse and learned quickly to evaluate patients' needs. She thought she might like to become a bedside nurse at home, one day—if the war ever ended.

A station hospital in the war zone was very different from the immaculate and orderly hospitals June had worked in back in the States. The sudden onslaught of large convoys of patients, the hurried triage, and the intent speediness needed in order to care for a large number of critical patients at once was unlike anything she had experienced before. The sense of urgency was overwhelming at times, but there was no time to reflect on it. While on duty, the doctors and nurses worked continuously, sometimes in silence, sometimes during pure bedlam. When off duty, they ate and slept.

Sitting in the tent after work, the nurses often took time to share the day's experiences, needing to put things in perspective before going to sleep.

"You know," June said one night, "I don't think that death is the most difficult issue we have to deal with here. Patients who have lost limbs, patients with head trauma that causes permanent disability, or all those patients with grave facial injuries, especially when they include the loss of sight or permanent destruction of facial features—I think those are the most agonizing cases for me to deal with daily."

The others nodded in agreement. Injuries to organs, causing lifelong pain and suffering for these soldiers, were common. After being stabilized, and sometimes after being operated on, the most severe cases were sent to the general hospital. During the winter of '43–'44, frozen limbs became the most serious issue. At the station hospital they would attempt to treat these conditions immediately. If the patient had gangrenous toes, the staff would begin by trying to get the circulation going. The one thing they were not to do was rub the patient's legs, and if the gangrene became "wet," the patient immediately had to be sent for more sophisticated treatment at the general hospital, and, assuming he survived, would most likely end up having the limbs amputated there.

The corpsmen helped the nurses with patients in the ward. There was Ward Master Sergeant Cleghorn, who told June he was from the South. Corpsman Jensen was another and was June's frequent sidekick.

*Sergeant Cleghorn, Ward Master*

One evening June was doing night duty in a different ward than the one she usually worked in when the corpsman on duty rushed up to her.

"Oh, June, one of the patients is hemorrhaging, please come quick, the doctor's not around." he said hurriedly, and led the way to the patient.

June checked and found the patient bleeding profusely. Her immediate reaction was to stop the hemorrhaging.

"Go find the doctor!" she said to the corpsman. Then she quickly removed the soiled bandages and put a pressure dressing on. While she waited for the doctor to arrive, she cleaned the bed and got rid of the soiled bandages.

"Nurse Houghton, what made you remove the bandages? Where did you put them?" the doctor asked.

June pointed to the bin where the bandages had joined other soiled ones.

"Now how am I supposed to gauge how much blood this patient lost?" the doctor asked angrily, as the bandages could not be distinguished from all the others in the bin. He shook his head and reprimanded her severely. June blushed, feeling foolish. She realized she shouldn't have disposed of the bandages, but this wasn't her usual department, and she wasn't used to the different routines here. She had just done her best, she thought. But even though she had helped—maybe even prevented something worse from happening to the patient— she had acted instinctively, without thinking. Well, she had learned something. She felt mortified, but not ashamed, and she was determined not to cry over it. She made up her mind never to feel pity for herself when chastised. Now she'd had two reprimands, the first one for arriving home late in London, and then this one. She would make sure there wouldn't be a third one.

# CHAPTER EIGHT

# WAR IN WINTER

September 12, 1943: Americans enter Germany.

September 8, 1943: Italy's unconditional surrender announced.

October 13, 1943: Italy declares war on Germany.

December 3, 1943: Roosevelt, Churchill, and Stalin meet at Teheran, agree on invasion plans.

December 24, 1943: Eisenhower named to command invasion.

January 11, 1944: FDR calls for a national service law to prevent strikes.

January 22, 1944: Allied troops land behind German lines at Anzio, near Rome.

January–May 1944: German operation Steinbock, the "Baby Blitz" in London.

It was to be a record winter, the first time in fifty years that they'd had snow in England. The winter of 1943–1944 was harsh all across Europe, with devastating cold and endless snow storms, and the 120th Station, as it turned out, was to remain in Malmesbury through two long winters. Most of the patients arriving from the continent had severe frostbites, often leading to gangrene and the loss of limbs, and even to the loss of life.

In the mornings, shortly after sunrise, the frost seemed to grow, expanding and glittering on grasses and branches along the perimeter of the field. The paths around the station were icy, and steam rose off the tents. It wasn't long before snow began to fall, gently at first, but soon the station was covered. The tent roofs were weighed down with snow, and the nurses had to take turns at getting up during the night to push the snow off the roof from the inside of the tent with a broom. The heat from the potbellied stove turned the bottom layer of snow on top of the tent into ice, making it hard to break and push off if they waited too long. They sincerely wished that they could ask one of those sturdy enlisted men to help, but since any "fraternizing" was against the rules, "fraternizing in women's tents during the night" would certainly not be tolerated.

When they woke up in the morning after the first snow, it had seemed to June as if they were living in a fairy tale. The whole world was white, and despite the potbellied stove being fed continually—indeed, it sometimes seemed to glow red—it was still chilly in the tent. The nurses soon got used to quickly shoveling their paths in order to get to work in the wards. Fortunately, they had gotten their winter coats and sturdy boots by then and arrived for work with rosy cheeks. The wards tents had two large stoves for heating and were tolerably warm, although not exactly comfortable. The most serious cases among the patients were put nearest the heat, and extra blankets were provided for those who needed it, pulled from storage. On the way to and from the wards, the nurses would sometimes stop in a protected spot for a quick chat and a few warm rays of the sun, but otherwise socializing was limited to evenings in the tent—as long as they were able to stay awake.

*Heater in patients' ward*

The chapel was decorated with sprigs of green for Christmas, and fervent prayers were said for an early end to the war. On Christmas Eve, the girls gathered around the potbellied stove, putting out the few goodies and cards received from home, along with mugs of coffee. Before she sat down on her cot, June turned the handle on the record player and with slightly trembling hand guided the needle onto the record. "I'll be Home for Christmas" caused even more tears than "We'll Meet Again" had earlier in the year.

June went to listen to Father Andre's telling of the Christmas message, and couldn't help crying as she sat there, thinking of all the men out in the fields of battle, cold and lonely, missing their families.

The winter seemed endless, with nearly all of the wounded now arriving with frozen limbs and pneumonia along with the ever-present war wounds. As soon as June arrived in the wards, she always warmed her hands by the stove before touching her patients. She found that the gentle touch of a warm hand would help calm a patient frantic with pain or anxiety. June had lovely, soft, well-cared-for hands, and sometimes a soldier would grasp her hand and hold it for a moment, until she gently pulled it away to stroke his brow, giving him a smile and a few encouraging words. June quickly understood that the physical touch was important to the wounded, who suffered both from physical and mental trauma. Often she lay sleepless in the night, worrying about her patients, until pure exhaustion helped put her to sleep.

June sat one evening next to a chest wound patient, who also was a double amputee. His legs were cut above the knee, and had begun to mend, to skin over. How strange those stumps looked, she thought, examining them. His legs look almost as though they had been made that way. The thin, new skin was soft and smooth, although still raw in color. The soldier woke as she went to put an extra blanket on him. It was getting colder outside, and the wind whipped at the tent flaps.

"You're healing very well, Joe" she said quietly, "probably won't be long before you get sent home now." Joe smiled at that

"You married?" she asked. Joe nodded. "Kids?"

"Two," he said. "Haven't seen the babe yet, she wasn't born when I left. The other one's a boy, he's four now."

"They'll be waiting for you. What were you doing for work before you came here?"

"Logging," Joe said. "Won't be doing any more of that, now."

"Maybe you'll get a job in the office?" June suggested.

"Maybe," Joe said, but he didn't sound convinced.

June wondered how the wife would take it. And the little boy, if he remembered his dad, would he be shy and frightened? Would he look at his father's stumpy legs and run away howling? The little girl would love him right off, June decided. He had such a nice, soft voice, and that friendly smile, and the baby wouldn't care about his missing legs.

Spring arrived, timidly at first. The 120th Station Hospital slowly turned from a Winter Wonderland to a mud swamp, and there was no time for lolling in a sunny, protected spot for a pleasant chat. The days were dark and seemingly endless, and they almost wished winter back. Then the trees began to bud, and hope returned. Pale green leaves sprouting shyly on the trees surrounding the edges of the station almost managed to engender optimism, as though a new beginning was possible. But the war dragged on, and the wounded kept appearing in long convoys of mud-spattered trucks.

*June used to bike to Long Street, Dursley*

When the spring thaw ended, and the roads were dry enough to be passable again, June sometimes took the bike for a ride into Dursley, near Malmesbury when she had time off. She always stopped by the Market Cross, an ancient landmark built around 1490. She was told it was built with stones salvaged from a ruined abbey. Market Cross is an elaborately carved octagonal structure that stands in an open square. The writer John Leland in his writings in 1540 described it as "a right costly piece of work" built to shelter the "poore market folke" when "rain cometh." It still served that purpose, and was most often referred to as "The Birdcage." If it was raining, June would lean her bike against one of the eight sturdy posts and stay inside the octagon until the rain stopped. It was a convenient meeting place, as you could stand inside and look out in all directions. It was also a nice place to rest and remember a different time, when there was no war and no injured soldiers waiting on her return.

*Another biking destination: Market Cross, Malmesbury Center*

# CHAPTER NINE

# GLOUCESTER, CIRENCESTER, AND SWINDON WILTS

March 4, 1944: US planes attack Berlin for the first time.

March 8, 1944: The plan for the invasion of France, Operation Overlord, is confirmed.

March 30, 1944: RAF suffers grievous losses in a huge air raid on Nuremberg.

April 5, 1944: Wendell Willkie withdraws from presidential race.

April 26, 1944: US Army seizes Montgomery Ward and Company in Chicago as a result of a strike.

May 6, 1944: Heavy Allied bombings of the continent in preparation for D-Day.

A ll leaves and furloughs had been canceled. The great invasion was imminent. In late May, June's unit was assigned to a staging area in Swindon Wilts for two weeks. Swindon, situated forty miles east of Bristol, was not far from Tortworth Court. Nearby was also Charlton Park, in Malmesbury, Wiltshire. While there, June got to meet the Countess of Suffolk, who lived at Charlton Park. The Countess's husband, the Earl of Suffolk, had been killed in an explosion in 1941 while on a bomb disposal mission in Kent, as always armed with his pistols "Oscar" and "Genevieve." The event took place in one of the "bomb cemeteries," where bombs were left on open ground in the marshes awaiting disposal. This particular bomb had been nicknamed "Old Faithful" as it had been left on the marsh for a long time. The explosion had killed the earl and two of his longtime working companions, along with eleven people who were nearby, including five sappers—combat soldiers who performed various military duties including bridge-building, laying or clearing minefields, and other tasks to aid the allied forces in moving forward. Later, Sir Winston Churchill reminisced:

> One bomb disposal squad I remember which may be taken as symbolic for many others. It consisted of three people, the Earl of Suffolk, his lady private secretary and his chauffeur. They called themselves "The Holy Trinity." Their prowess and continued existence got around among all who knew them and 34 unexploded bombs did they tackle with urbane and smiling efficiency, but the 35th claimed its forfeit. Up went the Earl of Suffolk in his Holy Trinity. But we may be sure that, as for Mr.

Valiant-for-Truth, all the trumpets sounded for them on the other side.

The earl had earlier spent time in France and Germany on some breathtakingly dangerous missions, earning him the nickname "Mad Jack." He had been charged with rescuing industrial diamonds and the entire world's supply of heavy water at that time. His wife Mimi, countess of Suffolk and Berkshire, who had now invited June into her home, was quite a personage in her own right. She was a former dancer and singer named Mimi Crawford (also known as Mimi Forde Pigott). The countess, who still lived at Charlton Park with her children, took an interest in June and introduced her to the duke and duchess of Gloucester. Lady Alice, duchess of Gloucester, a descendant of King Charles II, was married to Prince Henry, duke ofGloucester, and third son of King George V. During the war, the duchess was working with the Red Cross and was the head of WAAF (the Women's Auxiliary Air Force). When June met her, the duchess was the Air Chief Commandant.

One day, the subject of religion happened to come up.

"Oh, so you're a Catholic," the duchess of Gloucester said, and then she found out that June had never been confirmed. With all the disruptions of moving, family hard times, changing schools, and working and studying to become a nurse, there had never seemed to be time enough.

"Well," the countess said, "being part of the Catholic part of the royal family, we'll have to take care of that!" And so, the duchess set out to make the arrangements.

During the war, if someone hadn't been baptized, confirmed, or made first communion, this could take place. Due to the seriousness of the war, rites could be performed, no matter what religion—and there was a chapel nearby. June gladly accepted the offer and was promptly confirmed at St. Gregory's Chapel.

"Oh, thank you, you can't imagine what this means to me," June said to the duchess after the ceremony, grateful for her help.

The duke and duchess also took June to a historic area of Gloucestershire. Along the roads they traveled appeared miles of stone walls from ancient times. The great Gloucestershire Valley, through which the long, meandering river Severn flows, made a great impression on June.

"See those great willows overhanging the river? Hooked a pretty young salmon there last month," the duke said, pointing to a spot where the river took a turn and the water ran faster, casting a rainbow spray over the rocks. Willows and alders grew along the river, their roots sometimes exposed by the flowing water.

The valley's beautiful Cotswold towns and villages were home to Norman towers and ancient castles and abbeys, most often built out of honey-colored limestone. It seemed a serene and unexpected setting in the midst of a cruel world war. As they drove on, June admired the old churches, older than anything she had ever seen in her young home country. In the Catholic churches in this part of Britain, the walls had been plastered over after the reformation. "There are to be no more murals or statues of saints," the order had been, in the 1547 injunction against images. Stained glass, shrines, and statues had been destroyed or defaced. Roods and bells had been taken down; vestments had become prohibited. Stone altars had been destroyed and replaced by wooden communion tables. June was teary-eyed, imagining the loss of history and of the comfort in sitting among those old, familiar icons. Now, an effort at restoration had been started. In one church that June walked into, fragments of beautifully painted roses could be seen under the flaking white paint, and June felt that the roses might have been surrounding St. Teresa, one of her private favorites, and the saint her grandmother had been named after.

As June's unit was driven through the countryside, they found the main roads barricaded around Cirencester and Swindon. Barricades of different designs, some of them looking like old castle walls with pointed towers, had been built across roadways in the area in case Britain should be invaded by German tanks.

*Swindon Wilts. Streets barricaded to prevent German tanks from entering area*

En route to a parade in Cirencester, the 120th convoy was now forced to go by a roundabout way. When they finally arrived at the staging area, Queen Mary, the "Senior Queen," who was Princess Elizabeth's grandmother, was there to review the troops. Later followed another review, where the 120th had to march in a parade in front of General Patton. Some of the nurses were by now getting a little snappy. They were tired of parades and reviews and wondered when they would be going back to what they had come for, which they felt was caring for wounded soldiers. They didn't know that when they got their wish, it would probably be the most heart-wrenching and difficult time of their life.

*June's nurse unit marching. Inspection, parade, and review by General Patton*

While temporarily stationed in Cirencester, the 120th Station, along with other units, were fed in large mess tents. Shortly after the meal one night, all the soldiers and medical staff began to drop like flies. A great outbreak of severe diarrhea was discovered to have been caused by the cream of wheat, into which some temporary kitchen helper had inadvertently dumped washing powder from a cardboard box left on the counter among the boxes of cream of wheat. Severely dehydrated, the doctors and nurses had to treat both themselves and the rest of their unit. Later in the evening June and a few other nurses had dragged themselves out onto the lawn to sit in the fresh air, pale and exhausted.

"Well, at least we're all cleaned out," June said, but they were all too weak to laugh.

Back in Swindon, recovered from the unfortunate outbreak, the nurses found that there were homes designated all around the area—some quite grand—at which the people who lived there had been told that they had to take in a certain number of boarders during their stay in Swindon. June ended up living with three ladies who had agreed to take one boarder. The address was Seventy-Seven, the Mall, Swindon Wilts, in the home of what June came to think of as "the Three Graces."

"This is you room, dear," said one of the ladies, who was tall and thin and wearing a cardigan despite the summer heat. She opened the door and let June peek in. June thought the space must have been used as a closet, but they had managed to squeeze a bed into it, and a little night table with a lamp.

"Oh, that's very nice, thank you," June said. The ladies showed her around the house, which was warm and friendly, before letting her go to her afternoon duties. When she got back it was dark but the door was open, and she stepped inside, making a little noise so that the ladies would know she was back, and went to her room. In the morning she woke up with a start—surrounded, in that tiny, narrow room, by the Three Graces waiting to serve her breakfast in bed. One of them was carrying a little, white sheltie in her arms. Smiling, another one held out the breakfast tray. This became a daily routine while June stayed in Swindon.

*"The Three Graces" at Swindon Wilts*

Breakfast consisted most days of tea and a biscuit, and after that June had to go down to report in the center of Swindon Wilts. The unit had to remain in that location throughout the day; they were not allowed to leave the area. US paratroopers were milling about—in fact, the whole of Swindon was covered with nurses and American troops awaiting D-Day.

Toward the end of their stay in Swindon Wilts, Princess Elizabeth arrived to review the troops and paratroopers gathered there.

"She looks so young. Eighteen isn't she, but she looks like a lady," June said.

"But look at those shoes...and walking in the grass...I hope she doesn't take a tumble," Frances said. The princess was wearing a beautiful white coat and hat and high-heeled shoes. She walked out on the rough lawn very gracefully, despite her high heels, looking serious and determined.

"Oh, I hope she won't mind if I take a picture of her," June said suddenly. She had her camera along and quickly stepped out in front to get a photograph of the princess, who was accompanied by a highly decorated officer. The princess looked a little sad, June thought. But when she finally had the photograph printed, June found that just as she had taken the picture, the princess had flashed her a little smile.

*Crown Princess Elizabeth at Swindon Wilts*

# CHAPTER TEN

# BACK AT TORTWORTH COURT

June 4, 1944: Rome falls to the Allies.

June 5, 1944: Operation Overlord commences when more than one thousand British bombers drop five thousand tons of bombs on German gun batteries on the Normandy Coast in preparation for D-Day.

June 6, 1944: American, British, and Canadian forces land in France, D-Day. The Americans climb the cliffs and hills on Omaha Beach, suffering heavy losses.

June 13, 1944: Germany launches a V-1 flying bomb attack on England. The V-1 attacks continue through June, causing horrifying losses, especially in London.

August 8, 1944: Plotters in the bomb plot against Hitler are hanged, their bodies hung on meat hooks; reprisals against their families continue.

August 25, 1944: Paris is liberated; de Gaulle and Free French parade down the Champs-Elysees. The German military disobey Hitler's orders to burn the city.

Back at Tortworth once again, June's unit was soon put on alert. No one was allowed to get leave; everyone was confined to the station. June, waiting, got her camera out and took some pictures. Annie, Juanita, Marie, and Mary Ellen, a few of the new friends she had made, were smiling, all wearing their helmets. When they weren't at work in the wards, they spent time cleaning, working on the Quonset huts and the tents, inside and out.

"Look at me, I'm a chimneysweep," June shouted, as she was pulling herself up to the top of their tent to clean out the stove pipe, all the time hanging onto the rope with one hand. The officers had an enlisted man clean their chimneys, but no man was allowed into the women's area, so the nurses had to take care of their own.

"Watch out, or you'll fall off and break a leg"," Nellie shouted back.

*June acting as chimney sweep*

Meanwhile, they worried about what was going to happen next. One night they heard a mighty *roar, roar, roar*, and they all ran out of their tents. They stood there in the total darkness, and now they could vaguely make out huge shapes, large masses of them, up in the sky. June and the other nurses stood and looked up in amazement at a seemingly never-ending stream of planes. It was as if a gigantic swarm of locusts was on the way over them, headed toward the English Channel. What could they be? They had never seen anything like these planes. June knew that she would never forget that sound, or the image of those big, black shapes overhead.

What June and the others saw in the sky were the Gliders of Operation Overlord, attempting to liberate Europe. The Gliders spearheaded the invasion into Normandy. The Hamilcar, Horsa, and Waco Gliders were large, motorless craft, pulled by planes across the water only to be cut loose to glide down into Normandy, where they would crash-land and unload their cargo of men, vehicles, and arms.

The entire nose section of the Glider, including the pilot's compartment, swung upward to create an opening, which made it possible to unload the Glider quickly. The Waco Gliders carried combat men; jeeps with combat supplies and soldiers; howitzers with rounds of ammunition and artillery men; and small bulldozers. The great Hamilcar Gliders even carried tanks.

General William Westmoreland said afterward,

"It was a do-or-die situation for the Glider pilots. It was their awesome responsibility to repeatedly risk their lives by landing heavily laden aircraft containing combat soldiers and equipment in unfamiliar fields, deep within enemy territory, often in total darkness. They were the only aviators in World War II who had no motors, no parachutes, and no second chances."

The Gliders, along with tens of thousands of American, British, and Canadian forces, were aiming for Normandy on the coast of France. The next day, when the Gliders landed, near the Caen Canal and Orne River in Normandy, was June 7, 1944, D-Day. Seventeen thousand British and American paratroopers were dropped over Normandy, many of them drowning in flooded deltas. At the same time, arriving by sea, thousands of landing crafts were lowered into the water. Five thousand war ships and 1400 aircraft carried additional personnel and arms. Hours of heavy combat followed, in which thousands of Allied forces soldiers were killed.

At 9:17 on June 7, there was a press communiqué from the Supreme Headquarters Allied Expeditionary Forces of General Eisenhower, in which the world was informed of the D-Day invasion. At 12:00 noon, Prime Minister Churchill informed the House of Commons. The liberation of Europe from Nazi Germany had begun.

At the 120th Station, June and the other nurses listened to the astonishing news, as did the enlisted men.

"Better get prepared, girls. We'll have a lot of wounded arriving," Hazel warned, and they hurried to get ready for what was to come.

"Come on, make sure the supplies are refilled, and get the triage area set up," the order came. An enlarged triage area was prepared where medics would examine the wounded. Soon, ambulances began arriving in large numbers. The most seriously wounded were evaluated and stabilized and then immediately transferred to one of the ports used for transport back to the States. The intermediary wounded got sent to the general hospital. The remaining wounded were left at the station to be treated, operated on, and brought back to health and then, if possible, sent back to the front lines, reassigned to their units.

The 120th Station Hospital had doctors for every type of injury. Orthopedic doctors, surgeons, medical doctors—even neurologists to determine if there was any neurological damage. There was no psychiatric care. If a patient suffered from shell shock, which later was to be termed *post traumatic stress disorder*, it usually wasn't visible except in withdrawal, it was thought, and then the physician would have to evaluate it to find out if it was a "temporary symptom" or if the patient was really mentally ill. If a patient was found to need treatment, he would have to be sent home.

The Germans had carried out Operation Steinbock in January against Britain, but they were now running short of planes. Instead, German scientists had invented new weapons: V-1 flying bombs and V-2 ballistic missiles, which were now being used in a great aerial assault on London and other cities in the south of England. The British called this campaign "the Baby Blitz," as it was not as large or as destructive as the great Blitz of 1940–1941. However, the losses were horrific. June thought of her visits to London, a city already so wounded that she doubted it could ever be restored.

It was now June of 1944, and the arrival of wounded soldiers went on unabated into the fall and the beginning of winter. Most of the patients were English, Irish, Scots, Australians, and Americans, all part of the Allied Forces. The nurses saw a lot of night duty, and afterward they would have a reprieve and sleep in their tent for a couple of hours before going back into the ward.

June was tending a new arrival, who told her his name was Kelly. June smiled.

"That's a fine Irish name," she said, trying to make him feel good.

"I'm British," he retorted gruffly.

"And I'm American," she retorted, and the soldier chuckled. Smiling, June added, "and I'll take good care of you."

They also had a German patient, a Nazi Luftwaffe man, whose plane had gone down practically next-door to the station grounds, and he was therefore brought to them to be taken care of. He was severely injured and needed an immediate blood transfusion.

"We don't have a match," the doctor was told, after a rapid check of blood supplies. The soldier's blood type was rare, and a scramble took place to find a donor.

"Well, it seems I'm it," said Captain Finkelstein, when he turned out to be the only person in the camp who matched. Finkelstein, who was the Doctor in Charge at the time, was the chest surgeon in June's department. Captain Finkelstein's blood was a perfect match for the Luftwaffe man, and so they quickly transfused him. Afterward Captain Finkelstein stood quietly, looking at the patient with a slight smile on his lips.

"We will never let him know that he now has non-Aryan blood in his veins," he whispered. And of course nobody told the patient, who survived and was sent elsewhere. Wherever it was, no one would be able to tell him about the Jewish blood his veins were carrying since the only information in the paperwork was the type and crossmatch.

The arrivals of convoys seemed endless, with waves of wounded arriving from June into the fall, and then winter came. The Battle of the Bulge started on December 16, 1944, and would go on for a month. When word was out, June knew that new waves of wounded would be arriving. The patients from the Battle of the Bulge were American, English, Irish, and anyone else in the Allied Forces. They would arrive all throughout that long winter, day after blistering cold day.

*American patients from the Battle of the Bulge, outside the PX*

Snow fell relentlessly, covering the station and weighing down the tents. The nurses drew the tent flaps closed and kept the potbelly stove going, and still they were often shivering with cold. It was true that in the large ward tents the stoves were also larger, but every time someone entered or left the tent a great draft of cold air would blow through and the wounded would groan and cry out.

They were still dealing mainly with bayonet wounds, shot wounds, and injuries from stepping on mines, but most of the wounded that arrived after the Battle of the Bulge also suffered from frozen limbs. Many lost the battle after gangrene set in, and a great number of soldiers were left permanently disabled, doomed to spend the rest of their lives in wheelchairs—or, if they were lucky, with prosthetic limbs. It was a sad sight when these wounded left the 120th Station, carried off again on litters, loaded into ambulances, and taken a nearby port to be shipped off to the United States. June knew that even if they lived, most of these soldiers would never walk again. She tried to envision all these men living their lives in the States and hoped that they would be respected and appreciated for what they had done for their country.

One of June's patients, named James Gregory, had arrived with badly frozen feet. He remained a patient for a long time with his various injuries. The doctors worked hard to reverse the damage, and when James got back on his feet, shakily at first, he ventured outside, hobbling about slowly and carefully. One day he came across a squirrel and gave him some crumbs. After that the squirrel turned up every day outside his tent. James tamed him, and the animal became his constant companion, always sitting on his shoulder.

"Oh, Jim, wait, I have some nuts here that your squirrel might like," June called once, running after him. James stopped and took them. After that, whenever June saw this odd couple, she would run out with a few nuts or some other treat and put them into James's hand, as the squirrel would not eat out of anyone else's. At long last, when it was determined that his feet were saved, James was finally transferred to the United States for further treatment. The squirrel still came looking for him, but even though he was offered some occasional crumbs, no one could seem to take James Gregory's place.

*June with three American patients. James Gregory, behind wheelchair*

*Patient James Gregory with his tamed squirrel*

Another of the patients from the Battle of the Bulge was Sergeant Henry Terrell Dickey, NCO. Sergeant Dickey had arrived with a serious chest wound and had to be administered the new and painful penicillin injections. He went through a long, slow recovery, and June got to know the patient quite well.

"So, Henry, where are you from," June asked him the first time they chatted.

"Oh, way back, from Atlanta, Georgia. My dad was head of the Chamber of Commerce there. But when I left to come over here, I was a student at Holy Cross in Worcester, Massachusetts," he said.

"Oh, I'm from Massachusetts too," June said.

"Aha, I thought you sounded like it. Homesick yet?" Dickey asked.

"Well, sometimes. But I think you'll be back there before me," she answered. They had many conversations during his recovery. Sergeant Dickey was handsome and charming, but June was not ready to go beyond friendly small talk. It wasn't just that it was frowned upon; she knew she had to keep her head and her heart on the task.

When Sergeant Dickey was sufficiently recovered, he was transferred to join Crown Prince Olav of Norway (who would later become King Olav). King Haakon VII of Norway and Crown Prince Olav, along with the Norwegian government, had gone into exile in the United Kingdom after the German occupation of Norway. Crown Prince Olav, who became the Norwegian Chief of Defense, had been on a visit to the United States before the war and had formed a close relationship with President Roosevelt, which would prove valuable during the war. The Crown Prince made many visits to the Allied troops in the United Kingdom, and Sergeant Dickey, when fully recovered, joined Crown Prince Olav in what was later to become the Norwegian Disarmament of the German Occupying Forces.

*Sgt. Henry Terrell Dickey, center, and Crown Prince Olav, right*

# CHAPTER ELEVEN

# NEW ARRIVALS AT TORT-WORTH COURT

September 12, 1944: Americans enter Germany.

October 4, 1944: American forces break through the German Westwall.

November 7, 1944: President Roosevelt is reelected for a fourth term.

November 16, 1944: Allies launch general offensive on three hundred-mile front.

December 16, 1944: The Battle of the Bulge, or the Ardennes Offensive, is launched by Germany. For the Americans, the largest and bloodiest battle fought in World War II.

December 24, 1944: Americans halt the Nazis on the ninth day with help of seven thousand plane raid.

December 29, 1944: Russians penetrate into Budapest, Hungary, freeing it from the Nazis. On their arrival, the Russians arrest Raoul Wallenberg, who had saved tens of thousands of Budapest Jews from annihilation. Wallenberg is never seen again.

**A**ll of a sudden barbed wire was being put up all around the station. No one knew what was going on, and everyone was on edge.

"What's happening *now?* Are we surrounded and imprisoned? Have the Germans invaded England?" someone asked. Anxiety was rising. Finally, the entire hospital area and all of the tents had been completely enclosed by barbed wire.

"Get all the American patients ready to be transported out," came the order the following morning. And still, nobody knew what was going on. It was an unsettling, even frightening, time, and the nurses were filled with anxiety, while still carrying out orders by rote. Finally, all the patients were gone; the English had been transferred to general hospitals, the Americans sent off to whatever port could handle their numbers to be sent to the United States. The station was empty, surrounded by barbed wire, and no one was allowed to leave the grounds.

*Tortworth Court being surrounded with barbed wire*

One morning they could hear the roar and rumble of a great new convoy arriving, but this time it was carrying German prisoners. In September of 1944, the Allied *Operation Cobra,* led by General George Patton's Third US Army, had made a North–South breakthrough. One of the fiercest battles in the war was fought in Brest, Brittany. Brest was the westernmost port in France, and to capture it would mean having port facilities where the enormous amount of war materiel could be unloaded. It was estimated that the Allied forces would need 26,000 tons of supplies per day. Brest was surrounded and stormed by the US VIII Corps. The old city of Brest was razed to the ground and the port facilities destroyed, and so, in the end, Brest was of no use to the Allies. During the fighting, a hospital had been captured, and the patients and staff had now been shipped across the channel and on to Malmesbury and Tortworth Court.

The first arrivals at Tortworth Court were the hospital's German nurses and doctors. The 120th Station's status had suddenly been changed to a "Prisoner of War hospital." Hastily, June and the other nurses had to collect any clothing they could spare to give to the German nurses, as they had arrived with nothing but what they had on. The corpsmen, June assumed, had to do the same.

Later, the wounded German soldiers began to arrive. Soon the station hospital was filled with German prisoners, some seriously wounded. The German corpsmen, called "sunnies," were assigned to help the American staff. Some of the sunnies spoke English, but not many. Patients kept arriving, Germans, Austrians, Mongolians, Eastern Europeans; there seemed to be no end to the stream of wounded. Most of the injuries were from broken legs, bullet and bayonet wounds, and traumatic head wounds.

*German patient on litter, waiting for A&D Office assignment*

The Mongolian patients all carried their little prayer rugs along with whatever clothes they had. As a religious group, they had to be allowed to say their prayers. There seemed to be many very young patients from Bavaria, and June did not find them at all aggressive. She took pictures of two Bavarian soldiers who were only fifteen years old. "We didn't want to be in the German Army," they all professed. It was quite an experience taking care of those young boys, June thought. *They are young. They are seriously wounded. Yet, we mustn't think of them as "the enemy." Each one is a human being and must be cared for.* She felt that the medical staff had to tread carefully and stick to doing their duty as doctors and nurses. If not, they would be no better than Hitler's Holocaust doctors with their Final Solution.

One of the fifteen-year-olds had lost both his legs up to the knees after stepping on a land mine. June became quite attached to the boy, who said he had been drafted into the German Army against his will. A couple of the American corpsmen also became quite close to him and decided to keep in touch with him when he left. The patient was transferred to the States and fitted with prostheses, they later learned. When the patients were well enough to leave, they were divided up and sent off to prison camp. Some of them would be staying in England; others would go to the United States, others to Russia, where they would have to remain in POW camps until after the war.

Günter Dolle was a young Luftwaffe man from Germany. He was a chest patient under June's care, and June thought he was a nice young man. She proudly showed Hazel that he had given her his "wings," complete with an embroidered swastika, which he had ripped right off his uniform. Hazel shook her head.

"You're such a softie, June," she said, but June carefully wrapped and put away these items in her valise.

*German patient Gunther Dolle, eighteen years old*

*Gunther's wings, given to June*

When the weather allowed, the German soldiers were allowed outside to get some fresh air. They had all been given thick, navy blue robes and were lounging outside the tents, looking more like visitors to a health spa than prisoners of war. There was no rule about fraternization between Germans. The German men and women, although living separately, were allowed to meet and socialize around the wards A favorite pastime was "spazieren gehen," or *going for a walk*. Still, despite all the rules, there was often friendly conversation between the German patients and sunnies and the American corpsmen and medical staff around the wards

*German patients from Battle of the Bulge, wearing dark-blue robes*

One of the German sunnies by the name of Dietz was very helpful in the wards. He came from Cologne, Germany, and was well educated. The medical staff soon noticed that the German prisoners did not want to be handled by their own doctors and "Schwesters," as they called their nurses, but always requested to be treated by the American medical staff. June was curious to know why that was. She soon found out from Dietz that it was because the German doctors didn't use much anesthesia. With June's unit, the rule for the doctors was always to put a little Novocain around the area to be treated—if they were operating near the eyes, for instance—before they would put the needle in. Earlier in the year they had learned much about the uses of anesthesia and used whatever medical products they were able to acquire in order to eliminate pain. As soon as the German patients figured this out and managed to get treated by the American medical staff, the groans and loud cries that often had been heard from the German operating tents abated.

*German "sunnies" (medics). Fourth from left, Dietz, was a helper in the ward*

The 120th Station had received quite a number of injured SS Troops, and these patients had to be kept separate, as they were not allowed to be in the same tent with the ordinary German soldiers. June had one patient who was completely isolated, being a German officer from a high echelon of the SS Troops. He had probably stepped on a land mine, she assumed, because he had lost part of a leg and part of an arm and had bullet wounds too, along with chest wounds. June was not allowed go to tend to the SS Troops without her corpsman, Jensen, by her side. One day, June and Corpsman Jensen noticed the Iron Cross this important SS officer had received. The corpsman immediately wanted to take it from him, but June wouldn't let him. Not knowing that the officer could speak English, June argued with Jensen.

"No, Jensen," she said, "you can't touch that; that's his. He was awarded that."

"Well, but I'd like it as a souvenir," Jensen retorted.

"You're not getting it," June said. "That's his."

After a moment, the SS officer turned to June and said, in English, "That's very charitable of you. That does mean a lot to me."

June found out that the German officer spoke excellent English and was a very cooperative patient. He had to be, due to the helplessness caused by the lost limbs, and June never had a problem with him. Sergeant Warren brought men sent from headquarters to interrogate the SS Troops, and June met one of them, Lieutenant Ross, at the bed of this SS officer, and later at other beds of secluded patients.

When June told her friends about stopping Jensen from taking the SS officer's Iron Cross, they were a little taken aback.

"Well, I wouldn't want *them* to be able to do that to *our* men, would you?" she said. The thought did occur to her later that the Iron Cross might have been awarded for sinking an

American ship. That had caused her some anxiety, but she still felt that what she had done was right. When he finally left, the SS officer was sent to the States due to his serious injuries, where, assuming he recovered, he would be transferred to a POW camp.

There was one tent that was noisier than all the others. Sometimes a great ruckus erupted in there, and everyone wondered what was going on. Finally, June decided she had to find out. This time she purposely didn't take her corpsman along, as he would always stop outside to shout "Achtung" before they entered. This routine was to let the patients inside know that a nurse was about to enter their tent, a rule that was presumably meant to make sure that the patients were "decent." Every time the patients in that particular tent heard the call, they would immediately stop their chaotic noisemaking, and there would be silence.

This time, June sneaked inside quietly, without being noticed. One of the patients in the tent was a young man from Alsace-Lorraine, a section on the border of France and Germany, and he was the one getting the other patients upset. He was scrubbing the floors, which had to be kept clean in order to avoid infection, and while he was scrubbing—or really just mopping, as he wasn't allowed to exert himself too much—he was singing *La Marseillaise* at the top of his voice. That would get the German soldiers riled up, and soon they would be waving their bandaged arms in the air, banging their crutches on the floor or against the bed rails, and stomping their feet, shouting at him to stop singing. But he continued, cheerfully singing away, over and over, while he mopped the floor.

There was complete pandemonium in the ward until suddenly the men noticed June standing there, and a hush fell in the tent. The young patient put the mop by his side and looked defiantly at June, and she felt sorry for him. She thought, *oh, he's just a cute little kid—how can I reproach him?* And he was just a young French boy drafted into the German Army against his will; along with so many like him. Because he was so young, the staff tried to keep him busy mopping and doing light duties. June just shook her head, trying not to smile, and left. The boy was eventually sent to the United States, as he had a bullet in his heart that the doctors on the station couldn't get out. Meanwhile, he joyfully did all he could to aggravate the German patients in the tent. June suddenly remembered how the raucous men in the hospital ward in California had treated her and wished she'd had the gumption that this boy was displaying. Well, maybe she would develop it in time.

Another patient, an Austrian, was a very accomplished linguist. He spoke four or five different languages and they used him as an interpreter because of his language ability. He'd been assigned to Russia by the Germans—against his will, he insisted. His name was Wenard Parak. He had been a member of the SS troops when he was in the German army. In the evening, sitting in their tent, June was telling Hazel about him.

*Wenard Parak, young German soldier drafted from Vienna, Austria*

"When I first had him as a patient, I didn't know he could understand English, and of course he was in my section because it was all chest surgery for bayonet wounds and bullet wounds and so forth, so I looked at this fellow and I said to Jensen, my corpsman, 'Isn't he handsome? Look at those blue eyes and that red hair,' and I said, 'Putting that blue johnny on him sure enhanced the color of his eyes,' and as I was saying all this the fellow looked at me, and when I finished, he smirked and said, 'Thank you very much!' But he *was* handsome."

"Well, at least you didn't say anything derogatory."

"Oh, no. But he had beautiful red hair, and those blue eyes..."

"What were his injuries?" Hazel asked, shaking her head.

"Oh, a bayonet wound. And a bayonet wound, well, as you know, it doesn't look like much from the outside, because it's small."

"But if it hits an organ..."

"Right, or if it's twisted." They both groaned.

As Wenard got better, the nurses kept using him as interpreter, as few of the American corpsmen were fluid in German.

At long last, they got a sudden notice to get all their German prisoners—patients, doctors, and nurses—ready because the prisoners were going to be leaving. They had to assign a certain number of patients to go to the States, another number to England, and another number to Russia. Some were sent to hospitals for treatment, some to prison camps. And Wenard was to be shipped to Russia, which June was unhappy about, and she complained to Hazel.

"Well, do you know for sure that he was conscripted against his wishes?" Hazel asked, a little dubiously.

"Of course I do—you can just tell. Some of them are so young. And this fellow is barely twenty. His name is Wenard, and I've asked a lot of people, and they say it's a Czechoslovakian name. He himself says he's from Austria, but that his family came from Czechoslovakia. Oh, isn't it a shame, though?"

# CHAPTER TWELVE

# THE ARMY OF OCCUPATION

February 5, 1945: Third Army smashes through the Siegfried Line.

February 13, 1945: Budapest is liberated.

April 12, 1945. President Roosevelt dies of cerebral hemorrhage at Warm Springs.

April 16, 1945: Truman, taking office, pledges unconditional surrender, international organization for peace as his goals.

April 28, 1945: Mussolini and his mistress shot dead by Italian Partisans.

April 30, 1945: Hitler and his wife kill themselves in his bunker. Germany overrun by the Allies.

April, 1945: Buchenwald concentration camp freed by Allied troops.

May 8, 1945: VE-Day, Victory in Europe. Germany signs a capitulation.

June 26, 1945: United Nations Charter signed at San Francisco.

Now the camp was empty again, and their unit got orders that indicated that they were to be sent in Forty-and-Eight trucks to Ipswich, right on the English Channel.

"We'll get to see the Cliffs of Dover! But where will we go from there?" June asked.

As it turned out, there would be no time to go sightseeing. From Ipswich they were shipped across the Channel, ending up in Le Havre, France. They didn't know it yet, but this would be a seemingly endless journey through country after country on the European continent, all marred by unbelievable devastation. When they arrived in Le Havre, they found it completely bombed out. There wasn't a building standing, and the people were begging in the streets. It was a piteous sight. Shaken, they continued on and were finally housed in Rouen. June looked around at what she remembered was the site of St. Joan of Arc, now a place once again haunted by strife and death. June's unit was housed in tents outside Chateau Neufchatel, a tremendous castle that had been made over into a Red Cross hospital. They were fed twice a day at refectory tables in the cellars of the castle. To ensure that the castle wouldn't be bombed, a large red cross had been painted on the roof.

*Chateau Neufchatel, Rouen, France*

Shortly afterward they were sent on to Cherbourg, where they stayed for a short time before continuing to Marseille, on the French Riviera. They were billeted at a huge hotel, in what seemed like a bridal suite, about fifteen to twenty nurses in one room. Through the window they could see the harbor, where a number of warships lay at anchor. The streets were crammed with people; sailors, soldiers, and ordinary citizens mingling, looking for a place to eat or sit and enjoy the sun, as if the war had never happened. During the time they stayed in the hotel *Le Golf,* they were taken for daily drives around the country-side, through many small villages.

"Come on, hurry up, the bus is waiting," Nellie said one morning. That day they were taken to the Flanders Fields, a vast area filled with white crosses as far as the eye could see. The ground was still black with mud and soil, but June could imagine what the fields would look like once the grass grew.

"Oh, it's so sad, but think how nice it is of the French people to take such good care of all the fallen soldiers in this huge territory," June said, teary-eyed. At every Flanders Fields crossroad there was a little chapel with hand-painted plaques telling who had been killed or injured there, whether French or foreign.

*Marseilles, France*

By then Germany and the Allies were no longer firing on each other. June's contingent was to stay on the Continent until the latter part of 1945. The purpose of this long, winding transport was simply waiting to get members of 120th Station reassigned.

"Why do we have to go on this long train ride?" they asked, again and again, until they were finally told that it was to be decided who was going to be assigned to further duty in the CBI—the China/Burma/India contingent—where the war was still going on. While hostilities were winding down, the 120th kept traveling across Europe.

"We're like the *Flying Dutchman*," someone said, "unable to remain anywhere, just forced to go on and on." Going by train across France, they were still forced to travel only at night, and in the mornings the train would have to pull over. There were no bathrooms on the train, and as soon as it stopped, everyone ran for the latrines. If they took their helmet along, they could ask the engineer of the train to fill it with water so that they could wash their face. Sometimes they were on the train for several days and nights in the same clothes, and the stench of sweat became intolerable.

Once, as the day dawned, they pulled into a place where they'd have to stay until darkness. When they woke up and looked out, there was another train on a track opposite theirs. Looking into the windows of the other train the nurses saw hundreds of big, dark men wearing red fezzes.

"Where are they from? Africa? The shores of Tripoli?" Grace said jokingly. The men looked back at the nurses, who were a bit taken aback. For a while, the men kept staring, and the nurses stared back at them. *Who were they?*

"They must be POWs, since they don't leave the train," June guessed. She couldn't decide whether their stares were angry or sad, but she began to feel sorry for them, and her eyes teared. Surely, those men had been drafted into this war of horror just like some of the young boys from Bavaria and Czecho-slovakia and other places that they had been treating at the station. What could these men in their fezzes have known about Hitler's plans for humanity? None of the nurses wanted to step outside. Shortly afterward, as the POW train left the station, some of the men turned to gaze at them as they passed by. As soon as they were gone, June and her friends hurried to step out and hit the latrines.

Another time when the train pulled in to a station, the nurses hurried off to take care of their bodily needs. That done, they climbed onto another train parked on the next track, which they had heard was supposed to be carrying a lot of food. The train June's unit was traveling on didn't have anything much to offer, except for the C-ration packets, of course. The nurses had small containers that they could make lemonade in, using some hard crystals that came with the packet; and then there was the consolidated *something-or-other* (they didn't really want to know what it was, but they assumed it would have to include some kind of meat) that was supposed to have enough nourishment in it to get them through the day. June knew she'd never forget the lemonade and the little chunk of...whatever it was—something that was supposed to look and taste like ham, she thought—that was almost too horrible to bite into. The other thing that bothered them on the train was that there was no place for them to sit down to eat, no dining car and no tables. They made sure to eat their meals while they were not moving. Holding the drink in one hand and keeping the food from falling off their laps was too difficult on the moving train, which jolted along, often on uneven tracks, making sharp, squealing noises at every slight turn.

"Let's go check it out," the girls said eagerly when they heard about all that food on the other train.

"Look! Do you believe it? I haven't seen this much food since I was back home in Connecticut," Frances said.

"It reminds me of Market Day at home," agreed Grace. There was lots of food, and they gobbled up all they could. However, with the recent meager rations, their stomachs had shrunk, and this sudden excess of intake made them sick as dogs afterward. The stench in the car became unbearable again, and there was no other way for them to get cleaned up than to wipe their faces until they looked respectable and then go and beg the engineer for water to fill the helmet.

They were finally part of the Army of Occupation, and now the train could travel even in the daytime. Now and then, when the train was at a station, they were sent to take part in parades or other long and exhausting events and later transported in Forty-and-Eight trucks back to their unit again. One day June was presented with the following document:

## NURSES STAGING AREA
## NORMANDY BASE SECTION
## APO 562    US ARMY

SPECIAL ORDER
NUMBER 4                      31 May, 1945

1. The following named officers, members of the casual group, Nurses Staging Area, Normandy Base Section, will proceed to Paris, France, on TD for one (1) day, on or about 1 June 1945. Upon completion of TD, the officer will return to their proper. Govt. Motor T is authorized.

2. (Here followed the names of the nurses, one of them being June E. Houghton 2$^{nd}$ LT. ANC.

The paper was signed by Robert E. Owens, 1$^{st}$ Lieut. NAC, Adjutant.)

June would be going to Paris, and on her birthday, yet! But when it came time to leave, the quota had already been filled, and she wasn't able to go. One of her luckier friends later gave June a photo taken at the Arc de Triomphe, with all the soldiers and nurses celebrating the recent German surrender.

*Arc de Triomphe, Paris*

Eventually, the train crossed the border into Germany. On a rainy day, with a heavy mist hanging over the countryside, they crossed the Siegfried Line. The nurses crowded around the windows, perplexed to see what appeared to be pyramids in the misty, distant landscape. As they came closer, they found out that the pyramids were Hitler's tank traps—and, of course, in reality, they proved to be on a much smaller scale than the great pyramid at Giza. They reminded June of the barricades she had seen around Cirencester, although the shapes were different. They saw thousands of Hitler's "pyramids" planted across vast regions. The train relentlessly drove through the ravaged areas that had seen Hitler's final efforts fail. June wondered how the landscape, and the whole world, was ever to be restored. Equally dispirited, Hazel finally brought out the record player, and they played "We're Gonna Hang Out The Washing On The Siegfried Line," which made them feel better. They all sang along while looking out the window.

"Guess the laundry's all done," Grace said, giggling.

They were exhausted; all they wanted now was to get the word that they could go home. They read in the paper, which they could occasionally get a copy of, the daunting figures at the end of the war. Between September 1943 and April 1945, it was estimated that some 60,000 Allied and 50,000 German soldiers died in Italy alone, with the overall Allied casualties being 320,000. The Italian Campaign was the costliest in all of Western Europe in terms of lives lost and wounds suffered by infantry forces, and June thought of the convoys of wounded soldiers that had arrived to the 120th Station from that campaign.

# CHAPTER THIRTEEN

# WHEN THE LIGHTS GO ON AGAIN ALL OVER THE WORLD

July 15, 1945: Lights in Britain shine for the first time since September 3, 1939.

July 17, 1945: Truman, Churchill, and Stalin meet at Potsdam for final war conference.

August 5, 1945: Hiroshima blasted by atomic bomb, dropped by Army Air Force.

August 9, 1945: Atomic bomb dropped on Nagasaki. The Second World War ends with over forty million deaths.

October 24, 1945: The United Nations comes into being, designed to prevent future aggression.

November 20, 1945: Opening of the Nazi war criminals trials in Nuremberg.

*When the lights go on again all over the world*
*And the boys are home again all over the world*
*And rain or snow is all that may fall from the skies above*
*A kiss won't mean "goodbye" but "Hello to love"*
*When the lights go on again all over the world*
*And the ships will sail again all over the world*
*Then we'll have time for things like wedding*
*rings and free hearts will sing*
*When the lights go on again all over the world.*

Vera Lynn's voice was heard constantly on the radio, and the lights were truly on, even in London, which had been in the dark for so many years. However, the war was still raging in Southeast Asia. The Nuremberg trials were still in the future. Food rations would still go on into the mid-fifties in many European countries, but, finally, the war in Europe was over—although surely, new wars would follow.

Suddenly, the 120th Station Hospital got word that their unit was being sent home. Stunned and relieved, the nurses quickly started to pack up whatever they had left, by now mostly dirty and odiferous rags. Then they had to wait for their transport. At last, they were taken to a port on the northern coast of France, where June and her unit boarded the small Coast Guard boat *Marine Raven,* which would take them back across the Atlantic.

"Look at us, all squashed together," June said, laughing, on the first day of the crossing. It's certainly nothing like the voyage on the RMS *Queen Mary*."

At first they laughed at the difference; later most of them got seasick, June being one of them. It was a disaster, she thought, and not very funny anymore. There was no place to sit or lie down. Even getting to a bathroom was nearly impossible. They all stood around, slept in heaps, or sometimes fell asleep standing, leaning on each other. Finally, they worked out ways to take turns sleeping. A great cheer arose when they finally sighted the United States of America.

*On the Marine Raven, coming home*

When her unit landed in the States, after that seemingly endless voyage, June had to report immediately to Fort Dix, New Jersey. They had to stay there for about a week before they were allowed to go home. From then on, they had to report to Fort Dix every week and stay there every weekend before getting permission to go home. That went on until January of 1946. But even then they were not officially discharged. That did not happen until the war was officially declared over because June, as an officer, would be subject to return as long as that declaration was not made. Cessation of hostilities between the United States and Germany was finally proclaimed on December 13, 1946, by US President Harry Truman.

Until the long awaited discharge papers finally arrived, June spent some time pondering how to cope with her new situation. After three and a half years in the service—where she'd had people tell her when to get up, what her next duty was, when to go to bed, when to pack up and move—to find herself at home, where suddenly everything was so different from military life, was puzzling. She kept turning around, as if expecting someone to tell her what to do.

After a while, she decided to take off and go down to Florida to see her brother Warren. They had an emotional reunion before she returned north and went to visit some friends in Connecticut. Finally, she decided that it was time to settle down and *do* something. She went back to work at Cambridge City Hospital, as well as doing private duty at Boston City

Hospital. Early in the spring of 1946 she started at Boston University, studying surgical nursing.

The first time June had met Francis Sullivan was in 1939, when she was nineteen. Francis was the brother of one of June's classmates, and she had been invited to a Christmas party at her house. Francis, or Franny, as his family called him, had seemed nice enough, outgoing and sociable, she thought, but he hadn't paid much attention to her. She didn't see him again until after the war. While June served in the European Theater, Franny had been in the Pacific in the American Theater of Operations. Franny got back in the latter part of 1945.

Once June settled down, it turned out that she and Franny both had located in Cambridge, and both were working and going to college. They bumped into each other now and then on the bus. June soon found out that Franny lived just around the corner from her. She thought he was a handsome enough Irishman—the black, curly hair and those blue eyes flashing a quick smile at her. But he seemed kind of distant or—well, *nonchalant,* she thought. However, that handsome Irishman quickly became less distant and nonchalant. They began dating in January and by Easter of 1946 she had a diamond ring on her finger.

"Oh no," June said in alarm one evening shortly after their engagement, remembering that her confirmation had taken place during wartime in a church in England, one of thousands of rites and services performed for people of all faiths.

Franny looked questioningly at her.

"Well, will there be a record of it?" she said. In order to be married in a church, she would need it, and she definitely wanted to be married in a church. Anxiously, she sent a request to England. To her surprise, the certificate arrived promptly. On June 23, 1946, June Houghton and Francis Sullivan were married in St. Peter's Church in Cambridge. June was twenty-six, Francis twenty-eight.

*June and Franny's wedding, 1946*

June had saved up all her money while she was in the service and had enough funds to pay her own wedding costs. Franny's mother arranged to hold the reception at her house in Cambridge, and they were all grateful that it was a nice day. Afterward June found out that her husband was allergic to roses. And June had filled the house with roses!

For their honeymoon they went to a place in New Hampshire, near Woodstock. Franny was sick during the whole honeymoon, sneezing and coughing, all filled up. They spent their week there and returned to Cambridge, where they both promptly went back to work.

After they were married, they lived in a section called *Tar Paper Village*, a neighborhood of barrack-type buildings put up for veterans who couldn't afford to buy their own homes. In that day, a young couple couldn't afford to buy much, certainly not a house or a car. Sharing the same barrack was another girl and her husband. June and the girl had babies at about the same time, and then her neighbor's husband got a job in Gloucester, up on the North Shore, with the Beacon Oil Company.

"We're moving up to Rockport," her friend came and told them one day, and June was disappointed at the thought of losing her friend. The couple and their baby moved to Pigeon Cove in Rockport, a fishing village on the northern tip of the island of Cape Ann. Gloucester, on the south side of the island, where Franny spent much of his working time, was twice as large as Rockport. June knew she would miss her friend and the joy they had shared when their babies were born, but Rockport seemed awfully far away from Cambridge in those days, especially without a car, and the parting was tearful.

"Why don't you move in with me for a while?" Franny's mother, Anna asked, and after a while they did. Anna still had two children of her own at home, and June enjoyed living in a big, happy family.

Franny and June were both working hard and saving every penny and were finally able to buy a home of their own in Cambridge. By then they had three children. Maureen and Michelle, the twins, had been born in March of '47, and six months later, June had found herself pregnant again. A son, Kerry, had arrived in June of '48. They moved to a new larger home in Arlington in order to house their growing family. In September the same year, June went back and worked in delivery at the Cahill House at Cambridge City Hospital again and was still working there in 1952 when daughter Keva was born.

One day in 1955 June got a call from the old neighbor from the Tar Paper Village days. The woman and her husband were still living in Rockport, and she complained of feeling lonely, and of missing her old friend June. She had finally managed to look June up.

"Oh June, why don't you come up and visit? Bring the children, and we can go to the beach," she said.

Even though the brand new Route 128 was finished by then, it seemed a long and arduous ride, but at least now they had a car, and that summer June drove up there with the children—and by now she had four. That was her first time in Rockport, and it was *love at first sight*, she said.

Franny, being a seasoned sailor, had always loved the sea, while June had grown up without seeing the ocean until she was ten years old. But she had loved the sea ever since—both on the West Coast and on the East Coast—and that, combined with the friendly small-town atmosphere, was enough to draw them both to Rockport. They soon bought a small place in the little fishing village where, to begin with, they spent the warm part of the year. Franny and June both worked, taking opposite shifts so that one or the other would always be home with the children. In the summer, June commuted back and forth to Cambridge to work weekends and evenings, 11:00 p.m. to 7:00 a.m., and Franny worked days.

Franny was very smart, but due to the Great Depression, and then the war, he never got to finish college. While they were living in Cambridge after they were married, June encouraged him to go to Harvard in the evenings to get his electrician's license.

"You can do anything you want in life," June said, and indeed, Franny got his license. He still worked at the Navy Yard, now as a Navy Electrician First Class.

Franny was extremely persistent and soon became one of the top gyrocompass men in the Navy Yard. He had a friend named Jimmy George, and whenever a ship came in the two of them went as a team and worked on the compasses. After a while they were nicknamed "The Gold Dust Twins." June and Franny were staying in Cambridge that winter. She came home from work one day, finding Franny waiting for her, as usual. They had only one car, and when she got home from work, June would drive him to wherever he was called to be on duty. She drove him down to his ship, and Franny said he'd let her know when to pick him up. Then she returned home.

Two or three days went by, a week went by, and then two weeks went by. She still hadn't heard from Franny, and by then she had called the Navy Yard several times.

"I think you'd better call the Bureau of Missing Persons," they finally told her. By that time, June was getting frightened, and it got even worse when she was told that the Bureau of Missing Persons couldn't tell her anything about him. Then, at long last, she got a phone call from Franny.

"You can come and pick me up. I've just been catapulted off of a boat," was the first thing he said. Both confused and relieved, she asked where he was.

"I'm down in Rhode Island," was the answer.

June quickly got a babysitter, packed up, and went down to Rhode Island to pick him up.

"What happened to you? Where were you all this time?" June asked.

"Well, you see, as soon as Jimmy and I got on board the ship we were to serve, the ship went out to sea," Franny began to explain.

This took place during the Suez crisis in 1956, and the ship was patrolling up and down the east coast, all the way down to Florida and back again, and no one was allowed off the boat, nor had any messages been allowed to go back and forth, which was why the Navy Yard hadn't been able to tell June anything. But that would be Franny's life from now on, June realized, and he would always be on demand for that kind of service.

Franny frequently had to go up to Gloucester to service the Coast Guard cutter General Greene. It was always a big production and would keep him away for the whole day. Once, Franny came home from one of his jobs looking a little smug. He'd been severely chastised for the fee he had charged. "You b-d son of a b! Just for turning one screw!" had been the complaint. Franny had calmly responded, "Well, nobody else knew *which* screw!"

It began to seem a long ride to commute from Arlington to Gloucester all the time. June would pack enough for a day and night and take him to the ship. Franny and Jimmy George really were the top men in the field, and June was proud of her husband. On one occasion there was a *Mark four* or *Mark seven* (gyro compass) from Germany that wasn't working properly. Nobody else knew enough about Mark four or Mark seven compasses, so the Gold Dust Twins had to go and take care of it. It turned out to be a German ship that had found that their compass was not working properly, so they had pulled into the nearest port, which turned out to be Gloucester.

"You know, it seemed funny and ironic to be working on a German ship, even so many years after the war, but we took proper care of it," Franny said when he came home.

In 1958, Erin was born in Cambridge. Franny and June finally decided to sell the house in town and move to Rockport permanently. For the next four years, June was a full-time mother. In 1960, Eileen was born. Franny served during the Cuban Crisis in 1962. Brian was born in 1966, when June was 46. At the time, they were living in a house on Broadway in Rockport. June was upstairs resting when her pains came on with a vengeance, and she called for the ambulance. The crew came up the stairs and helped her onto the stretcher.

"Oh, you can't carry me down those stairs, they're too narrow," she said. "And I'll slide off the gurney, they're so steep!" The men just smiled and brought her downstairs, taking the corners easily, disregarding any moans. They made it to the Addison Gilbert Hospital in time for Brian's birth. In 1968 June and Franny moved into a bigger house in Rockport. The home sits near Mill Pond, at the historic location of Rockport's earliest settler, Richard Tarr.

June had begun to work at the Addison Gilbert Hospital in Gloucester in 1962, once the family was completely settled in on the island. She started out working in South 2 Surgery and Medicine. In 1980 she went back to school to get certified to work in the Cardiac Care and Step Down Telemetry department. She became Charge Nurse in charge of the floor and worked in the First Cardiac Care room, a fourteen-bed cardiac care in the department of ACLS (Advanced Cardiac Life Support.) She loved her work, and sometimes contrasted the years working at Addison Gilbert Hospital with the years at the 120th Station Hospital. The war-time years had been a valuable beginning of a long career in nursing. Never again had she seen the chaotic working conditions they had lived through during those years in the war. True, even at Addison Gilbert, there had been emergencies and critical situations, but they had seemed like slow-motion movies in comparison.

In 1992, after thirty years at Addison Gilbert Hospital, June retired. She still kept her hand in as a nurse, doing blood pressure clinics once a week. In 1991, June had also started filling in as a substitute in the Rockport Public Library children's department, and later, after her retirement from the hospital, she also substituted at the main desk. In 1993 she took on the position of Outreach Librarian at the Rockport Public Library. June continued working at the library until 2009, when she decided it was time to *really* retire—just around her ninetieth birthday. That was also the year June decided to give up her driver's license and to take the bus to do her shopping and get to her appointments. The one thing she would not give up was her registration as a nurse. "You never know when you'll need it," she insists. At ninety-two, after seventy years, June is still a registered nurse, filing every two years. She also takes courses in medicine and keeps up on new treatments and medical findings.

# CHAPTER FOURTEEN

# HEARING VOICES FROM THE PAST

Prohibition. Women's right to vote. The Flapper era. Lindberg crossing the Atlantic. Bubble gum. Sliced bread. Penicillin. The discovery of Pluto. The completion of the Empire State Building. The Dust Bowl. The Hoover Dam. Organ transplants. World War II. Credit cards, color TV, computers. Polio vaccine. Discovery of DNA. Hillary climbing Mount Everest. The Civil Rights movement. First man in space. The Berlin Wall. Peace Corps. MLK's "I Have a Dream" speech. Assassinations. More wars. Opposition to wars. The Hippie era.

June's life now spans nearly a century. *The War,* as June thinks of it—as if it were the only one—is seventy years in the past now, but ever-present in her mind, right under the surface, available for contemplation. She can hear it, any time. The murmur of the men in the tents, chattering in the accents of the Allies: Australian, Canadian, Irish, Scots; or later, the sometimes incomprehensible babble of the POWs: German, Russian, Middle Eastern. The whistling of the wind in the winter, tent flaps clattering. The roar of planes overhead, and the distant whistle and boom of bombs. Moaning Minnie. The smells of war: iron and blood and gunpowder, sweat and musty clothing, ointments, cleaning solutions, coffee brewing on the potbellied stove.

In her mind, she can still *see* the war, too: soldiers' faces taut with pain; hair unkempt; bristle of beard on chins. Men lying limp and still, lost in their own world; others desperately reaching out for anyone walking by. An interpreter suddenly needed, and when not available, the soldier has to point to the pain and grimace. Patients shivering in the cold. Nurse's running down icy paths to get to the wards, teeth chattering. Wounded men arriving suddenly in large convoys, most of them needing urgent care—nothing like the comparatively orderly, steady trickle in a city hospital. Despite having worked as a nurse in hospitals all her life since those long-ago days, June knows that there has been nothing that could compare with working in a war zone. Maybe it is because the wounds of war were caused by what men did to each other, and in the days of World War II, most often by men within arm's reach and eye to eye.

It's seven o'clock on a rainy morning. A group of women sit around June's kitchen table, five librarians from the Rockport Public Library. Some of them are retired, some still active. They think of themselves as *The Library Group*. They have gathered here every week for the last fourteen years. The group expands at times to include other members or friends of the library, retired or active: Steven Rask, the former library director; children's librarian Ray Bentley; cataloguer Boyd Coons—the last two now passed away—and others. In the beginning, they used to take turns having the coffee hour at each others' houses, but June said it would be so much easier for her if they could meet at her house all the time, so she wouldn't have to leave early to go and bring her grandson Dan to the school bus. (Grandson Dan is now in college.) The other members of the group went along, promising to bring small contributions to the table.

When they arrive, the table is set: English china cups, decorated with roses; individual teapots, each under a tea cozy; toast and marmalade. Then the American additions: pumpkin bread with cream cheese, individual crystal cups overflowing with berries of the season, grapes, nuts, and dried cranberries. Flowers from the garden make a centerpiece. Being the unsurpassed baker and the "mother" of them all, June sets a table that would put a country inn to shame. Also waiting on the sideboard are individually wrapped treats to take home: slices of the day's cake or bread, or June's special "healthy" cookies (made with real butter but "not much" sugar). Feeble efforts are occasionally made by the visiting librarians to provide support for the table: cans of pumpkin for the bread, flour, sugar, dried apricots, coffee grounds, sausages, and cheese.

June takes her seat at the head of the table and passes the offerings before the general discussion starts. Usually, they begin by catching up on the last week's events.

"The library's been busy. Probably the weather. You're still missed at the library, June," Jane says, "and your outreach patrons are always asking for you, you know."

June's Outreach Librarian's list of books always included several new large print titles for the retired crowd that she served, as well as *Talking Books for the Blind*, tapes that were supplied by the NLS (National Library Service) for the Blind and Physically Handicapped. There were also books available in Braille.

"Oh yes, I miss them, too. I remember one couple I served, the Moores. They were elderly, you know, and Mrs. Moore always told me to just walk in and drop the books on the hall table so she wouldn't have to come down. She'd wave to me from the top of the stairs. Must have been at least seventy-five, poor old thing," June says. Everyone laughs at this, knowing June had been at least ten years older than "the poor old thing" at the time. June looks a little startled.

"June, she was a lot younger than you!" Diane says in explanation.

"Oh, dear. Yes, I always seem to forget how old I am. Must be the onset of senility," she says, laughing, a high-pitched girlish titter, and rubs away a tear that creeps down her soft, pink cheek. Her hands are still beautiful, sleek and soft, the fingers straight and unmarred by time. Her light brown locks are silvery now, surrounding a still young face. There are lines in it, but in that lively face, with those aquamarine eyes flecked with sea-green, and the ever-present smile, the lines seem to disappear and an eternally young woman emerges.

June uses her computer daily, having learned the basics during her early library years. To keep up with all the new programs, she went to the *Rose Baker Center for Seniors* in Gloucester for classes. Her children, especially her son Kerry, help her deal with new applications. She keeps up with old friends on e-mail, and occasionally finds news or information that brings memories of World War II days back. After the group has finished discussing the news of the day, local, national, and worldwide, there usually follows the awaited period of reminiscing. They like to listen to June, who has a lifetime of stories to tell.

"I often wonder what happened to some of the people from the old days. Oh, did I ever tell you about Celia?" she asks this morning.

"Wasn't she the one in the iron lung?" someone tries.

"Yes, that was Celia. At the South Department. Well, I found out not long ago—there was an article online—that she remained in the iron lung for twenty years. Can you believe it? Imagine spending twenty years...ooh, it's too hard to even think about it. You know, once she learned to gasp for breath, she could stay out of the iron lung for a couple of hours a day—

and later on, after I left, for several hours—but she always had to return to the iron lung. She could even go on short outings and to the theater. Then, after twenty years, when they invented the portable respirator, she was able to be moved out of the iron lung permanently. Prior to that invention, the patient had to live their whole life with the iron lung. To support herself, Celia read aloud onto tapes for the blind and sold magazine subscriptions. She was quite a lady, and so smart."

June shows a printout of the article, which has a picture of Celia in an oval frame, a lovely looking young woman with dark hair piled up on top of her head. Then, as she often does, June goes to get her World War II album and starts leafing through it.

"Oh, here are the Three Graces. That's what I called them. I was boarded in their home in Swinton Wilts. They always brought me breakfast in bed." And perhaps that's where June learned to set the breakfast table, even though June's breakfasts there had been brought to her on a tray. The librarians get the feeling that the scene in front of them looks just as though the Three Graces had appeared to welcome them to a proper British tea. A little more luxurious than in wartime, of course.

"The Three Graces and I kept in touch after the war, you know, until the last one died," June continues. "They sent me two little baby dresses that they had knitted for my girls. I have one still, hand-knit silk, I had it preserved and framed. The other one was made of wool, but it fell apart eventually." June turns the pages in the album, and stops, putting her hand across a page, pointing at a picture of a great mansion.

"This is Tortworth Court. You can see what a grand place it was. That's where I spent most of my time during the war, with the 120th Station. Can you believe it? They've since turned Tortworth Court into a place for mentally disturbed people. A lot of things changed in England after the war. But people there were so generous about sharing their homes and land while the war was going on."

She turns another page, and suddenly looks very sad.

"A long time ago I found out something about one of my German patients in England. His name was Wenard Parak— you remember, that young SS trooper who got sent to Russia at the end of the war. I know I've told you about him. Here's a picture of him. We had treated him for a serious bayonet wound. Well, sometime after I came back to the States I had a letter from Wenard's sister, who was studying to be a doctor in Austria. She sent me Wenard's obituary. After he got to Russia, according to her letter, he was made to sleep outside on the ground and developed tuberculosis. Oh, I felt so sad and worried when he was sent off. They didn't treat those patients very well. And then, when he got so sick there, they just sent him home to die. He came home from Russia weighing only 80 lbs—can you believe it? Anyway, at that time letters that were sent to people in the States were still censored, and so was the letter to me. In what was left that you could read, Wenard's sister told me that he died at home in Austria with his family around him. Oh, you know, he had red hair and the most beautiful blue eyes, and the first time I saw him, he was wearing a blue johnny, and I joked with my corpsman and told him that the patient was so handsome with those blue eyes and that matching johnny. That's when Wenard winked at me and thanked me for the compliment, and that was how we learned of his language ability."

"You like men with blue eyes, don't you, June," Linda says, teasing June a little.

"Oh, dear, but there was no one like my Franny. Oh, he had the bluest eyes…" June reaches for a tissue, and everyone laughs.

"What about your children, June? Did any of them go into the service?"

"Why, yes. Kerry was in the army. He went to Vietnam and signed up for extra time. I think that must have been a difficult war to be in," June says thoughtfully. "And especially the homecoming. There wasn't much appreciation or encouragement for our soldiers when they returned from Vietnam. It's been hard for him to deal with sometimes. He left college after Vietnam, but he went back later. He got his electrician's license at first, like his father. Then he switched and became a teacher. Finally, he studied and became a lawyer. Now he works as a lawyer for the state, for the Care and Protection of Children.

"Well, then there's Brian, my youngest. He was quite artistic as a child. Used to spend time with the Stanton boys, you know, the ones who created "Finding Nemo" and all those other movies. They used to hang out and draw cartoons together. They still keep in touch now and then by e-mail I think. Brian's a navy commander now. I went to visit him and his family a few years ago, when he was stationed at a naval air station in Sicily. His family was living in Paterno, which fell to the Allies while I was stationed in England. Driving around that area where they lived, which was near Mt. Etna, was a shock. To see how much damage from the war remains even now, after all these years of rebuilding, was very sad. And I couldn't help thinking of all those wounded soldiers who arrived at the 120th Station in England from Sicily.

"Now, about Brian...at one point he wanted to come out of the service because he wanted to see his children grow up in Rockport. I said to him that I really think people have to learn how to cope with different situations in their own life. In the long run, it makes them stronger and more able to face things in the future. That's the way I feel, that all these different things that happen in our lives teach us to live through difficult times. Coping with being in the service was hard itself. People asked me, 'What did you think of it as a young girl in the service in the middle of war?' I told them I didn't even think about it. You didn't have time to think about it because you're just there. You go with it. So, as I say, I think difficult things in your life teach you to cope with future problems. That's how I learned. I was reprimanded, and it was so difficult that I made up my mind to learn my lesson and never let it happen again."

"So Brian stayed in the navy?"

"Yes. He's served in the Baltic, and he was in the Gulf War for nine months. He's a lawyer now, like Kerry. He works with a law firm in Boston and lives here on the island. All my children live here, I'm glad to say.

"Let's see now. Michelle, she became a teacher. She's also very artistic—you see all her stitchery around here, and she's quite a gourmet cook."

"She takes after you, then," Diane says.

"Oh, no, I'm no cook. I'm just a baker," June says humbly. The librarians all giggle, knowing better.

"And what about Keva?" Jane asks.

"Keva is a teacher, too, and very smart. She's a sensitive girl, but not at all nonsensical, if you know what I mean. She'll be stopping by here for coffee after you leave. And next we had Erin. She was a paralegal, worked with a Gloucester senator on political and environmental issues. Now she is a selectwoman in Rockport. And then it was Eileen's turn. She's got a degree in geography. She is a personnel director at Gorton's in Gloucester—you know, *"Trust the Gorton's Fisherman,"* June sings the jingle. "Now that her children are off to college, Eileen spends much of her free time with her ah...somewhat elderly horse, Durgin."

June is proud of her family. It's a big clan now, as befits her Scottish ancestry: seven children, seventeen grandchildren, and six great-grandchildren. The great-grandchildren are all boys, but "not one of them a Sullivan," she complains. Over the years, June also took in foster children, who still come and visit with their families. Sadly, Maureen, the elder of June and Franny's twins, died of cancer a few years ago.

June turns a page in the album.

"Here's another German patient...see, on the right, in the wheelchair. He sent a letter to one of our corpsmen who got in touch with me. He was a young fellow, only fifteen, and he had lost both his feet. Actually, he was a Bavarian soldier who had been drafted into the German army. You know, he was one of those kids who were conscripted against their will. Well, even the Pope was conscripted into the Brown Shirts when he was little. Anyway, my corpsman had become very friendly with him, and that young fellow was sent to the States. He lost both his legs up to the knees, and he got prostheses in the States. Well, he always kept in touch with corpsman Jensen, who was a Mormon from Utah. After the war was over, Jensen and another corpsman went to Bavaria to meet up with him, after being invited to his wedding to be his best men. And they kept up their friendship for years, because on our reunions, this young man… well, he was our age…this Mormon from Utah, he would give us an update on this fellow's condition. He would go back and forth from the States to Bavaria to visit him."

*Corpsman Jensen, left rear, went to wedding of patient on right, who lost both legs*

"So this prisoner was the one who was fifteen? And he lost both legs up to the knee?" Diane asks.

"M-hm, yes. If I remember correctly, he lost them when he stepped on a land mine."

June lets them study the picture in her album.

"And that's my corpsman Jensen, on the left in the back, behind the wheelchairs."

On another page, June points to a snapshot of an American soldier in what looks like a beautiful garden, where roses are in full bloom.

"Oh, this is Sgt. Robert Gardner. Bob was an A&D (Admissions and Discharge) officer at the 120th Station. This picture was taken in the rose garden at Lilford Park. Now, Bob Gardner and his wife used to come up to Rockport and visit me every summer until about ten years ago. They'd stay here with me for a week. But they can't make it any longer. It's been a while since I heard from them. Oh, that was such a lovely rose garden at Lilford, but of course we never really had the time to enjoy it." June flips a few pages in the album.

"Here we are on the little *Marine Raven*, headed back to the States. *New York City, here we come.* You should have heard us when we sighted land. The *Raven* was nothing like the *Queen Mary*, as you can see. You know, Churchill once said that the *Queen Mary* shortened the war by a year." June turns another page.

"And here is Henry Dickey, the sergeant who joined Crown Prince Olav, the prince who became King Olav of Norway later. Sometime after I came back home I received a package from him. Henry Dickey, I mean, not King Olav. When I opened it I found a beautiful necklace with a blue stone. He was so grateful for his care, he said. He was very handsome, Henry, and had a nice way about him. You could tell he would go far. Well, when I got the necklace, I didn't think too much about it at the time—I mean, it was pretty, and I loved it, of course, and was touched that the soldier had remembered me. I put it away in my jewelry box. Then, recently, I took it out and looked at it, and I brought it to a jeweler and asked what the stone was. And the jeweler's eyebrows went up, and he said, 'This is a very fine aquamarine, and it's untreated, which makes it valuable. You should take good care of it and keep it in a safe place.' Can you believe it?" June is teary-eyed again.

"Well, Franny must have been pretty jealous when you got that gift," Linda says.

"Oh, no. Franny never needed to be jealous, and he knew it," June says, smiling, with a faraway look. It is many years now since her beloved Franny died. June cared for him herself at home during his long illness. She has shown the group one of the last photos she took of him, with the latest little grandchild cuddled next to him in the living room bed where he slept.

The hour is up. The group clears the table, leaving June, as always, with the dishes.

"No, no, girls, you're all so busy. I have all day," June insists, after passing out the "leftover" goodies (neatly wrapped in foil before the group arrived) to bring home. Well, they all know that June is probably busier than they are. At least they will help put things away, they insist. Finding a big pile of damp cloth on the bottom shelf of the refrigerator, Diane looks a little concerned. Has June made an "elderly mistake," and put her laundry into the refrigerator? June notices Diane's perplexed look and laughs.

"Oh, that's the church laundry. I'm just keeping it damp."

June recently decided that she needed a new refrigerator. Kerry asked what was wrong with the old one and told her that the new one she had decided on was too big, and asked what she needed a new one for, anyway. What about having the old one fixed? June said there was something wrong with the gaskets, and it would cost a lot to have it repaired. Kerry answered, laughing, "So it would be cheaper to pay over a thousand dollars for a new refrigerator than to repair the old one?" But June's daughters encouraged her, and said, "Go ahead, Mom, get a new fridge." Of course, when the delivery men arrived with the new fridge, it wouldn't fit through the door. Kerry measured the doorway and gave them a call, and they said they'd be able to take the doors off the refrigerator and get it in. Meanwhile, June still has to keep the church laundry damp. She has thoroughly cleaned and emptied the old refrigerator, and doesn't want to put any food back in it again, so the laundry reigns supreme.

Doing the laundry for St. Joachim's Catholic Church in Rockport is one of the many things that keep June busy. As the group leaves, they often see the large pile of white linens heaped in a clean corner of the kitchen. June has been doing the church laundry for years, following strict church specifications. The linens stained with the consecrated wine may be rinsed in the sacrarium, a special sink in the church with a pipe that goes directly into the ground, as the remnants of consecrated wine must not go down an ordinary drain. (The sacrarium is also where the priest washes his hands after the service.) The alternative is for June to rinse the linens at home in a basin filled with water that she empties right onto the ground, and that's her method. She starts by soaking the cloths. Then she treats the wine stains and removes any wax by gently scraping, and then ironing, the wax with a warm iron from the back until it has melted onto a layer of paper towels. She also carefully removes any lipstick marks with liquid dish detergent. Afterward, the linens are washed in a mild, unscented detergent, sometimes with an addition of peroxide, before the basinful of water is poured out onto June's side lawn and the linens hung to dry. When the linens reach the proper dampness, she puts them in the refrigerator or freezer overnight, which will give them a shiny, crisp surface when ironed.

In the morning, she steam irons the cloths from the back, so that the embroidery will stand out. Then she irons them gently from the front, but without steam. There are rules about how to fold purificators, altar cloths, corporals, and other linens, and Father Gariboldi is very strict about June following these rules. The purificator is first folded in thirds (using the fingers, not the iron) with the embroidery on the outside, and then again in thirds, so that when the cloth is turned over, the cross appears in the center of the square. And the folds must be done in the proper order, so that when Father unfolds the cloth, it will open correctly. Once the linens are done, June brings them to church and puts them neatly in the drawer.

Apart from laundering the church linens, June has held the position of Eucharistic Minister at St. Joachim's, and is involved in the church in many other ways. At the annual mass held in the church for her husband Franny, she decorates the altar area with flowers—but none of them roses, since Franny was allergic to them.

# CHAPTER FIFTEEN

# THE LEGION

And then, new wars, with American soldiers again in harm's way, and American nurses, again, there to care for them.

It's Thursday again, and the librarians step into June's fragrant kitchen.

"Mm-mm, do I smell German coffee cake?" Diane asks.

"Yes, and I made it with apricots, not raisins." She knows that they all love apricots.

"And what is that monstrosity over there, pray tell?" Linda asks, pointing toward the back wall of June's kitchen.

"My new fridge. What do you think?" June beams proudly. "They were able to fit it through the door, just as Kerry said. Thank goodness for Kerry. He can organize anything."

Tea and coffee poured, the members of the group sit down and dig in.

Memorial Day Weekend has just been celebrated, a big day for the American Legion in Rockport. June has marched in the parade—over a mile-long, uphill trek—every year until this year, when it was just too hot. Instead, she got a ride in an open car driven by her son Kerry.

*June at Memorial Day Parade 2012*

The parade route was lined with people waving, and as the procession of marchers and cars came to an end, the people, as always, fell in behind and marched along up to the cemetery. During the services, June stood, in uniform, behind the podium, along with Kerry and various dignitaries, while her youngest, Navy Commander Brian Sullivan, gave a moving speech in front of the large crowd. The Legion parade draws a big crowd every year and ends with convocation at a pier in Sandy Bay, where a wreath is thrown onto the water.

"So, June, when did you join the Legion?" Jane asks.

"Oh, dear. It was the milkman got me into it," June says.

"Now, that sounds very suspicious!" Linda says, raising her eyebrows, and the group laughs.

"Well, you know what I mean. This milkman was very friendly," (they all laugh again) "and he knew I'd been a nurse in the war and all that, and he asked if I belonged to the Legion. Well, his brother was one of the head men of the Legion in Boston, you see. So, I joined in Cambridge in 1947, and then when we moved to Rockport, I was automatically transferred to the Legion here."

"Back then, was the Legion in the same place that it is now, the same building down on Back Beach?"

"Yes, in that building. We fix it up a little now and then, of course."

"And is it still lively, would you say?"

"Well, we have a meeting every month. We'll be having a cake sale this Saturday, and we hope to earn enough money to have our Veterans' day in June that will bring veterans who are hospitalized, or living in Veterans' homes, and some of them don't get out at all. We bring them down from Bedford and Chelsea."

Linda gets up and puts the toaster on for extra time. They all like their pumpernickel toast dark and crunchy, with a little cream cheese on top, and maybe a dollop of lingonberry jam.

"So, you have veterans of other wars in the Legion, too, right?"

"I don't know if we have any World War I veterans left...," June says, hesitating a little.

"Oh, I don't think so. It was on the TV the other day that the last veteran of World War I just died," says Jane.

"Oh yes, that's right, and he had been only about seventeen when he went in...," Diane adds.

"So he'd lied about his age...," Jane assumes.

"That's right," June nods. "Happened a lot back then. But we still have people from World War II, from the Gulf War and Korea, and from Vietnam. Of course, now we're getting them from Iraq and Afghanistan too. Last year we had over a hundred veterans who came down for the day. For those who are able to go out in the fishing boats, the fishermen in Rockport donate their boats and time to take any veteran who is able to go out fishing. They bring them out and they fish, and whatever they catch they can bring back to the hospital or place where they live. Those who can't go fishing, who are wheelchair-bound or not able to face being out on the ocean, they stay and have coffee and share memories at the Legion Hall. People bring all kinds of baked things for them to enjoy. I remember Veino Jacobsen used to bring Nisu, you know that nice Finnish coffee bread made with cardamom. The Women's Auxiliary makes up lunches for all of the ones who are going out in the boats, so that each veteran is given his lunch; and they also make lunch for all of the veterans who stay here at the Legion Hall. Some of them are able to walk around town on their own. Those who can't go on their own, because let's face it, we have some who have to have a companion with them—"

"You mean like someone in a wheelchair?"

"Not only that, but some might take off and wander. They have a volunteer helper with them from the hospital or veterans' home that they are from, and they can walk around or go across the street from the Legion and just sit on a bench and watch the ocean. Those who are able can go around and walk downtown, even get a cup of coffee and then…in other words, have a nice activity day. And then we have a big main meal for them. The main meal is at about four o'clock, and that's when they all come back to the Legion, where we put on the big evening meal. Then, when they're finished eating, they have to get on their buses. In the past—up until five years ago—we were able to send goodies home with them, but we are not allowed to do that anymore."

"Why is that?"

"I think it's because of packaging…we can't donate our goods to them anymore. Oh, they used to love the take-home stuff, but we can't do it now. "

"The Legion also does a lot of things for people who are not veterans, right?"

"Oh, yes. We lend walkers—I just got through lending someone a walker, and canes to a couple of people…"

"Oh, I remember when you showed me that cane with the dingaling hanging…"

"Oh, yes, in fact, I was hoping I could get that one back so I could have it with me in the parade. But then I didn't get to walk, after all." They sense the regret in her voice.

"What about crutches? In fact, I have a couple of crutches from when I hurt my ankle—would you like them? You take donations like that from people. Is that how you get them?"

"Anybody who calls up and says, 'I've got this or that; could you use it?' Well, I don't think we've ever refused anything because if we find we can't use it, then we take it up to the recycling. And somebody is sure to pick it up there. You know how everything there finds a new owner. But generally we have a lot of...for instance, walkers. I've got a walker out there right now that I've got to get back. We even have wheelchairs. We lend quite a few of them.

"There is one wheelchair that does have a restriction on it. It's an electric one, and it's a good one, and the person who donated it said that he didn't want it to go to anyone except a veteran. That's all at his request, not at ours. And it's a very expensive one so that any veteran who needs it, we save it for them, but for other people that need one, we have other good ones. I've lent one out to one of the parishioners because her daughter was down here for the summer, and she has multiple sclerosis, and she couldn't get around unless she had this wheelchair. So she's had it the entire summer. I not only lent out a wheelchair, but an old tub shower seat and a walker, and it was out for over a year. It was for a grandmother who was very elderly, and the mother and the girl were taking care of her at home, so she had it for a whole year."

The World War II photo album comes out. On the first page there is a photograph taken a number of years ago at an annual meeting of the Legion, showing a large number of people.

"So do any of the people you knew in the war still come to the Legion event every year?" Jane asks.

June laughs softly, and the group realizes that most, if not all of them, must be gone. It doesn't stop June, however. She has been a member of the Legion since 1947.

"When you think of it, there possibly aren't a lot of people left in my age group, because at ninety-two, I'm one of the oldest ones that belong to the Legion," she says, simply.

"Okay, anyone for more coffee? Need more hot water for your tea?" Jane, trying to get past a sensitive moment, is getting the coffee pot. The women are into the little individual fruit bowls by now. Grapes are getting crunched; strawberry juice drips down the chins.

"Have you had any contact with the people you knew, the nurses or doctors you worked with during the war?" Linda asks.

"Oh, yes. The last reunion we had was about two years ago, and I forget where that one was held…we used to try to have a reunion just about every year, but I didn't start going to them until maybe twenty-five or thirty years ago. I didn't go to all of them, but I did go to quite few. Everyone would do something different. I hosted a reunion one year here in Rockport, and the people who came to it stayed up at what is now the Sandy Bay Motor Inn. I hosted them from when they arrived here on a Tuesday, and they left on a Sunday."

"That was a long reunion."

"Well, some of them arrived on Tuesday and some came later, but they all left on Sunday. Through the graciousness of Mr. Madruga, who owned a bus company in Gloucester, we had a bus donated to us. We only had to pay for the gas, which wasn't too bad, back then. Mr. Madruga even went to the airport to pick some of them up. So we transported the ones who needed transport to come here, and we transported people to the different places where we had arranged entertainment for them, such as whale watches and fishing and then sightseeing, like over to Hammond Castle and Beauport. They had a marvelous time because a lot of them were from the Midwest—Utah, as I said. We had quite a few Mormons in our outfit because many of the Mormons are conscientious objectors and don't take part in fighting, but they did take part in nursing during World War Two. The Midwesterners were just absolutely amazed at the greenery of this countryside because they came in July. Well, of course, they had come from a place that was hot and dry then. And they had a marvelous time. I forget how many people we had, but it was a large number. For the main meal, Franny had rented a big tent, and Janice and George Ramsden put on the big meal for them."

"Do you remember the nurses you worked with in England—were they all from around here?"

"Well, we did have some nurses from Pennsylvania and Connecticut. And a couple of the girls were from Raleigh, North Carolina. Grace Russell, she was from Maine. And Frances Melle was from Connecticut. That comprises most of my friends among the nursing personnel. A lot of the doctors were from New York."

"How about your closest friend of the nurses that you knew?"

"Oh, Hazel Hearn, she was from Connecticut. Ironically enough, when I moved here to Rockport I met up with her brother, who lived in Gloucester."

"So did they ever come to these reunions?"

"Oh, yes, they all came. They did."

"Did any of the doctors ever show up at the reunions?"

"Oh, yes, they came too. Some of the doctors did, and one of them actually showed up here at my reunion in Rockport. He was an orthopedic surgeon, and he was Italian, so he was very excited about the reunion being held here, right next to Gloucester, you know, because of the Italian section there. He went there and chatted with people in Italian, around the pastry shops and restaurants, especially. You can still find people to speak Italian with in Gloucester, but not so many of the first generation anymore. Well, this doctor was in our unit, and he was very happy to come, and I chatted with him. I wish I could remember his name, but I can't. It was an Italian name, but not one that I was very familiar with...he might have been from New York."

June remembers them all, the people she worked with; the patients; and the kind English people who generously shared their homes with their own countrymen in need of a safe place to stay during the war and who also welcomed the American nurses and soldiers into their homes when they were out on bivouacs, parades, and reviews. Most of all she remembers the patients. All she needs to do is close her eyes, and she can look straight into their eyes and hear their voices. She can stand by them to take their pulse and listen to the rain hitting the tent while somebody is telling a joke off in a corner, making everyone laugh.

Once she has cleaned up the kitchen after her guests leave, June will probably take Gertrude and go downtown. No, Gertrude is not her dog—the dog's name is Lily. Lily is a great guard dog, a tiny, white, fluffy thing. She barks at everyone walking by, especially if they are walking a dog. But she barks loudest of all at the mailman, who doesn't mind a bit. No, Gertrude is June's new toy, shiny red and waiting out on the sidewalk, fully charged and all set to take for a spin. Gertrude is one of those nifty wheeled vehicles that quite a number of the elderly or handicapped in Rockport are whizzing around on.

At ninety, when June gave up her driver's license, she started taking the bus to go shopping, to get to the doctor's office, and to do her other errands. Rockport, being just a small town on the northern part of the island of Cape Ann, no longer has a grocery store, so June has to go to Gloucester to do her food shopping. The city of Gloucester occupies the southern part of the island, and has supermarkets and chain stores and local stores galore. But Rockport still has a pharmacy, a hardware store, clothing stores, coffee shops, restaurants, and convenience stores, not to mention all those Bearskin Neck art galleries and artisans' shops, bakeries, and a brand new, and very grand, Symphony Hall. And let's not forget churches—Rockport has a lot of churches. June takes Gertrude for a daily ride. She makes a stop at the coffee shop, and then she drives around to get what she needs, drops it in Gertrude's basket, and zooms back home.

# AUTHOR'S NOTE:

Along with the author's personal interviews with June, the following sources have been found most useful:

## SELECTED BIBLIOGRAPHY

Kieran, John, ed. *Information Please Almanac 1948*. N.p.: Doubleday and Company and Garden City Publications, 1948.

McCollum, John H. *History of the South Department, Boston City Hospital, Infectious Service.* Boston, Municipal Printing Office, 1906.

Viets, Henry R. "Boston City Hospital: Its origins and early history." In John Byrne: *A History of the Boston City Hospital* (1905–1964) Boston, The Sheldon Press.

"Article XXI—Report of the Committee of Internal Health on the Asiatic Cholera, together with a Report of the City Physician (Dr. Henry G. Clark) of the Cholera Hospital." *American Journal of the Medical Sciences*, July 1850.

Prizer, Morris. "South Department." In John Byrne: *A History of the Boston City Hospital* (1905–1964) Boston, The Sheldon Press.

Goodwin, Doris Kearns. *The Fitzgeralds and the Kennedys.* New York, St. Martin's Press, 1987.

Kennedy, Rose Fitzgerald. *Rose Fitzgerald Kennedy: Times to Remember.* Garden City, New York, Doubleday, 1974.

O'Brien, Michael. *John F. Kennedy.* New York, St. Martin's Press, 2005.

Gray, Scott F. *The Little Book of Facts about the Big Ship.* N.p.: Trade paperback, 2003-2005.

U. S. Army Medical Department, Office of Medical History. http://history.amedd.army.mil/

Winston S. Churchill. *Their Finest Hour*. Boston, Houghton Mifflin Company, 1949.

Bennie Benjamin, Sol Marcus, and Eddie Seiler. *"When the Lights Go On."* 1942.

## ILLUSTRATIONS

Images gathered from June Sullivan's WW II album, along with private family photo albums and recent photos by author.

Reuben Goossens. *"The Gray Ghost at Sea"* www.ssmaritime.com/mainpage.html

*"The Gray Ghost, New York Harbor"* Wikipedia. (Public domain photo)